eSPeCiALLY FOR:

....

FROM:

....

DATe:

....

MARILEE PARRISH

GOD'S BEST FOR ME

180 INSPIRING DEVOTIONS FOR KIDS

SHILOH kidz
An Imprint of Barbour Publishing, Inc.

ISBN 978-1-64352-203-6

Published by Shiloh Kidz, an imprint of Barbour Publishing, Inc., 1810 Barbour Drive, Uhrichsville, Ohio 44683, www.shilohkidz.com

Our mission is to inspire the world with the life-changing message of the Bible.

Member of the
Evangelical Christian
Publishers Association

Printed in the United States of America.
06730 1119 SP

HI, FRIEND!

Did you know that God has great plans for your life? Yep, it's true! Kids have always been very important to Jesus, and He wants you to know how loved you are and that He made you for a purpose.

Check out this really cool verse in the Bible: "At that time Jesus said, 'I praise you, Father, Lord of heaven and earth, because you have hidden these things from the wise and learned, and revealed them to little children' " (Matthew 11:25 NIV). God wants everyone to trust Him the way that kids do! Your faith is so special to Him!

With a little help from my own kids, Jessa and Jake, who are almost eight and almost twelve, we've come up with some very important things that we believe God wants kids your age to know.

I hope you'll come along with us every day for the next few months as we find out what those great plans are!

With joy and excitement,
MariLee, Jake, and Jessa

FIRST THINGS FIRST

For God so loved the world that He gave His only Son. Whoever puts his trust in God's Son will not be lost but will have life that lasts forever.
JOHN 3:16

God loves you so much! That's the first and most important thing you need to know. You can accept Him or reject Him; the choice is yours alone. It's not a family thing like saying you belong to a Christian family (although following Jesus as a family is totally awesome!) . . .it's a personal, individual decision to accept God's love and choose to follow Him.

When you decide to follow Jesus, He sets His very own Spirit in your heart. He comes to live inside you and gives you supernatural power to follow Him all the days of your life. You don't have to get all cleaned up and perfect before you come to Jesus. He forgives your sins and accepts you just as you are. Take a minute right now and decide how you want to live your life. With the power of Christ—or without? Nobody can make that choice but you.

God, I accept Your love for me. I choose to follow You. Please forgive my sins and show me how to live for You.

*For God did not send His Son into the world to say
it is guilty. He sent His Son so the world might
be saved from the punishment of sin by Him.*
JOHN 3:17

Some people think that God is an angry guy who came to spoil all our fun. But Jesus didn't come to earth to point fingers at all the bad people and leave us to try to figure out how to be good. No! He came to help. God is not angry with you. He sent Jesus to take the blame for all the sins of everyone. His death on the cross for you made that possible. Then He rose up from the grave, and He conquered death and sin for all time.

Jesus came to make you right with God so that when God looks at you, He sees the righteousness (the rightness, the perfectness) of Jesus. You are clean and free to live a great life, with Jesus guiding you and blessing you.

....

*Wow, God! You see me as perfect because of
Jesus? How awesome is that! Thank You for
Your love and sacrifice for me. I love You, God!*

TRUTH SETS YOU FREE

"You will know the truth and the truth will make you free."
JOHN 8:32

God wants you to know the truth about who you are and who He is. He has so much to say about this in His Word, the Bible. He very much wants you to believe it and live like you believe it. Ask Jesus to help you believe these words as you read them:

- I am free and clean in the blood of Christ (1 John 1:7; Galatians 5:1).
- He has rescued me from darkness and has brought me into His kingdom (Colossians 1:13).
- I am a precious child of the Father (Isaiah 43:7; John 1:12; Galatians 3:26).
- God sings over me (Zephaniah 3:17).
- I am a friend of Christ (John 15:15).
- Nothing can separate me from God's love (Romans 8:38–39).
- God knows me intimately (Psalm 139).
- God is for me, not against me (Romans 8:31).

Knowing who you are in Christ will change your whole life forever.

God, thank You for telling me the truth. I choose to believe Your truth. Help me live my life for You.

Since you want to know, I will prove to you that Christ speaks through me. Christ is not weak when He works in your hearts. He uses His power in you. Christ's weak human body died on a cross. It is by God's power that Christ lives today. We are weak. We are as He was. But we will be alive with Christ through the power God has for us.
2 CORINTHIANS 13:3–4

These are some really important things to remember as God's child:

- God loves you so much that He sent His only Son for you (John 3:16).
- Jesus is God in a human body, completely God but also human (Colossians 1:15 and 2:9).
- God wants to speak to you in many ways.

God has unlimited power, and the ways that He can speak to us are also unlimited. He will often remind you of a scripture or a worship song that comes from His Word. He speaks through His creation and through His children, and in so many other ways. How does God speak to you?

....

God, thank You for Your love. I want to hear from You in any way You want to speak.

THE ONLY WAY

*After they had made fun of Him, they took the
coat off and put His own clothes on Him. Then
they led Him away to be nailed to a cross.*
MATTHEW 27:31

Psalm 145:17 (NIV) says: "The LORD is righteous in all his
ways and faithful in all he does." We are not. We sin.
We mess up. We've all made lots of mistakes. We can't
understand everything about God or His ways, but we
do know that we can't get to God if we aren't perfect.
That's why Jesus came!

God made us and loves us so much. But He made
each of us with the ability to make our own choices. We
can choose to live in our sins, forever separated from
God. Or we can choose to accept the righteousness
(perfectness) of Jesus and be with God for eternity.

Jesus died to take our sins so that when God looks
at us, He sees the perfect sacrifice that Jesus made for
us instead (see 2 Corinthians 5:21). Jesus came and died
so that we can be made perfect before God. It was the
only way.

*Jesus, thank You for making a way
for me to be with You forever.*

A GOOD WAY TO PRAY

Jesus said to them, "When you pray, say, 'Our Father in heaven, Your name is holy. May Your holy nation come. What You want done, may it be done on earth as it is in heaven. Give us the bread we need everyday. Forgive us our sins, as we forgive those who sin against us. Do not let us be tempted.'"
LUKE 11:2–4

Jesus wanted to show His followers how to pray. Of course, you can talk to God about anything and in any way. This is just a great example from Jesus.

He started off by praising God. When we worship and praise God first, it helps us to be thankful. Then we ask God to meet our needs. Needs are very different from wants. Prayer is a two-way conversation, not a wish list we're giving to God. Then we ask for forgiveness for mistakes we've made that might be getting in the way of our friendship with God, and we offer forgiveness to others. And finally, we ask for God's spiritual protection.

....

Jesus, thank You for teaching us how to pray.
I'm glad my prayers matter to You.

TALKING TO JESUS

Because of this, God lifted Jesus high above everything else. He gave Him a name that is greater than any other name. So when the name of Jesus is spoken, everyone in heaven and on earth and under the earth will bow down before Him. And every tongue will say Jesus Christ is Lord. Everyone will give honor to God the Father.
PHILIPPIANS 2:9–11

A few years ago, Jake woke up in the middle of the night, upset because he had a bad dream. Have you ever had a bad dream that wouldn't stop playing over and over in your head? What worked for Jake might work for you too!

First you need to know that God hears your prayers and that the name of Jesus is very powerful. Jake asked Jesus for help with his bad dreams. He told Jesus about the monsters that he saw and how the dream made him feel. And you know what Jesus did? He gave Jake a new picture in his mind of Jesus turning all the monsters into things Jake loved instead. When you are afraid, talk to Jesus. Say His name. He will help.

. . . .

You name is powerful, Jesus. You make the darkness and fear disappear.

A HEALTHY REST

*I wait for the Lord. My soul waits
and I hope in His Word.*
PSALM 130:5

Do you feel like you're always in a hurry? Many people always seem to be in a rush to get to the next thing. It's a rush to get to school or church on time, then sports practice or your after-school club. . .we are running, running, running. Lots of activities aren't bad. . .unless they are distracting you from God.

Did you know that God took a rest after He created the first week? The Bible says He blessed that day and made it holy (Genesis 2:1–3). Did the God of all creation need a rest? No, He is God! But He rested as an example for us to follow. God wants us to rest from our work and our activities. He wants us to create space for Him in our lives.

God, help me to slow down and focus my plans on You. Remind me that You're always with me during all my activities, but help me to take a real rest from all of that so that my body and my mind are healthy, the way You designed them to be.

I'VE GOT THE JOY

You will show me the way of life. Being with You is to be full of joy. In Your right hand there is happiness forever.
PSALM 16:11

God promises to fill us with His joy—and we don't have to wait until heaven for that! We have access to His peace, joy, and presence right now while we live on earth. The Holy Spirit alive inside of us will show us the way.

Hebrews 4:15–16 (MSG) says: "We don't have a priest who is out of touch with our reality. He's been through weakness and testing, experienced it all—all but the sin. So let's walk right up to him and get what he is so ready to give."

How cool is that?! Just walk right up to God, and He will fill you with peace and joy in His presence. Joy is much different than happiness. You can have supernatural joy even when you're sad about something. Joy is a firm hope that good is coming because of Jesus (check out Romans 15:13 too!).

God, I ask that You would fill me with joy in Your presence. I want Your constant presence in my life and the joy that only You can give.

GROWING UP IS HARD WORK

*Dear friends, your faith is going to be tested as if
it were going through fire. Do not be surprised at
this. Be happy that you are able to share some of
the suffering of Christ. When His shining-greatness
is shown, you will be filled with much joy.*
1 PETER 4:12–13

Growing up in this crazy big world can be hard. Jesus Himself told us we're going to have trouble here, so we shouldn't expect it to be easy. But He also said, "Take heart! I have overcome the world" (John 16:33 NIV).

So how can we live with joy in our hearts while we're expecting trouble? Well, we wake up each morning expecting some challenges, and we ask Jesus to help us through each and every one. This doesn't mean you have a negative attitude, expecting the worst. Instead, you can look at trouble as a challenge that you can conquer with God's power. We can find Jesus in each hard thing, and He will give us joy in His presence!

*Jesus, I know there will be some challenges today,
but we can get through each one together. Thanks
for helping me and strengthening me as I grow up.*

THE TRUE LIGHT

This true Light, coming into the world, gives light to every man. He came into the world. The world was made by Him, but it did not know Him. He came to His own, but His own did not receive Him. He gave the right and the power to become children of God to those who received Him. He gave this to those who put their trust in His name.
JOHN 1:9–12

When the Bible says "man," it's usually referring to mankind or all people. And that includes you, whether you are a boy or a girl. This verse means that Jesus is the light and He brought His light to all people. If you accept Jesus and allow His light to glow in you, you become a child of God.

John 8:12 (NIV) says: "When Jesus spoke again to the people, he said, 'I am the light of the world. Whoever follows me will never walk in darkness, but will have the light of life.' "

God wants to help you live in the light. Ask Him to help you shine your light in dark places.

. . . .

Jesus, thank You for filling my heart with Your light. Help me to carry Your light with me wherever I go.

RIGHT AND WRONG

The Laws of the Lord are right,
giving joy to the heart. The Word of
the Lord is pure, giving light to the eyes.
PSALM 19:8

God doesn't give us rules and guidelines to make us unhappy or to spoil our fun. He doesn't tell us right and wrong so that we'll be miserable our entire lives. Nope, our God is a good dad. He's the perfect parent. And just like wise parents set rules and good boundaries for their children, God has given us rules to help us enjoy life better and keep us from danger.

In fact, the Bible says that God's rules give joy to our hearts and light to our eyes! When we follow God with all of our hearts, He leads us where He wants us to go. Proverbs 3:6 (NLT) says, "Seek his will in all you do, and he will show you which path to take." This is the best way to live!

....

God, I thank You for teaching me right and
wrong. I know it's because You love me and
want to keep me from danger. Help me to
respect Your plan and enjoy following You.

HOPE FOR THE FUTURE

The Lord will give strength to His people.
The Lord will give His people peace.
PSALM 29:11

You're going to have tons of decisions to make as you grow up. And sometimes life can get pretty confusing. But the Bible tells us that "God is not a God of disorder but of peace" (1 Corinthians 14:33 NIV). He doesn't want you to be confused but to have peace that He has your future in His hands. He knows exactly where you're going to be ten, twenty, thirty years from now, and He knows exactly what you'll be doing.

Whenever you feel confused and you want to know God's will, just ask! God's Spirit inside you will teach you and show you His will as you seek Him in each moment. Get into God's Word and you'll get to know His will even better. A great verse to memorize is Jeremiah 29:11. Look it up! God knows the plans He has for you, and they are to give you a hope and a future.

God, help me make decisions that honor You as I grow up. Please give me the desire to get into Your Word and know You more.

PEACE ALL THE TIME

*May the Lord of peace give you His peace
at all times. The Lord be with you all.*
2 THESSALONIANS 3:16

We're going to talk a lot about peace in this book. God's very best life for you includes the peace that only Jesus can give. Jesus says this: "Peace I leave with you. My peace I give to you. I do not give peace to you as the world gives. Do not let your hearts be troubled or afraid" (John 14:27).

What does *peace* actually mean? When people who don't know Jesus talk about peace, it usually means they want quiet and a time of no problems. But Jesus says that He isn't talking about the kind of peace the world wants. It's been said that God's peace isn't the absence of trouble but the presence of God in the midst of trouble.

Peace is about the presence of God. . .no matter what kind of situation you face—good or bad. It's trusting that God has the very best planned for you, even if bad things happen.

....

Thank You that I don't have to be afraid even when bad things happen. Fill me with Your peace, Lord Jesus.

HELP WITH SCHOOL

"The Helper is the Holy Spirit. The Father will send Him in My place. He will teach you everything and help you remember everything I have told you."
JOHN 14:26

Jessa came home from school with a headache. She had so many things she needed to remember for school: new spelling words, a science test, homework. She felt like her head was going to explode. Have you ever felt like that?

Did you know that Jesus can help you with all the things you need to remember? His Spirit is alive inside of you, and one of His jobs is to help you remember all the things you need to know. Instead of getting upset and frustrated by everything you have to remember, ask Jesus for help.

Learning and getting your schoolwork done is part of growing up. And God is with you. He knows all the answers to every question you are learning about. He can help you with every single question and problem if you let Him.

....

Jesus, thank You for caring about everything I'm learning. Please help me remember what I need to know so that I can do my best in school.

GO AFTER THE RIGHT STUFF

*Turn away from the sinful things young people want
to do. Go after what is right. Have a desire for
faith and love and peace. Do this with those
who pray to God from a clean heart.*
2 TIMOTHY 2:22

You probably know kids your age who are obsessed with some of these things: screen time, the best games, money, clothes. . .and a lot of other "things" that don't really matter. Some kids think they'll only be happy if they have the next best thing. But here's the truth: Obsessing over "things" will never fill you up and make you truly happy. Only God can do that.

Did you know that there is a God-shaped hole inside of you that only He can fill? It's like a puzzle piece: He's the only One who can fit in that "joy" spot you have inside of you. So ask God for help to turn away from the wrong stuff and to go after His plan for your life. It's the only way to find true joy.

. . . .

*God, please forgive me for being obsessed
with the wrong things. Fill me with true
joy as I get to know You more.*

FRIENDSHIPS AND FITTING IN

We have spoken the truth. We have God's power. . . .
Some men respect us and some do not. Some
men speak bad against us and some thank us.
They say we lie, but we speak the truth.
2 CORINTHIANS 6:7–8

Do you find yourself trying too hard to fit in with other kids your age? Do you worry about what other kids are saying and thinking about you? When God's power is at work in you, you can be confident in who you are as His child no matter what anyone else thinks.

When other kids whisper about you or leave you out, that can definitely hurt. But as you talk to Jesus about your feelings, He reminds you of the truth. You are a dearly loved child of the King of kings! You have access to all of God's riches and knowledge. You can go boldly before the throne of God because of how loved you are.

. . . .

Lord, please forgive me for trying so hard to fit in
when You want me to be myself. Who I am in You is
what matters most. I pray that You would help me
to find good, Jesus-loving friends to hang out with.

*The Lord came to us from far away, saying,
"I have loved you with a love that lasts forever. So I
have helped you come to Me with loving-kindness."*
JEREMIAH 31:3

This verse in Jeremiah gives us a true picture of who God is. He loves you with a love that lasts forever. God is good and He is kind. When you mess up, He doesn't want you to hide in shame. He wants you to come to Him and let Him help you get it right.

Conviction is when the Holy Spirit inside you tells you that you've done something wrong. God convicts you gently and He draws you to Himself with His love and kindness (Romans 2:4). He is a most holy God worthy of all our respect and honor, but He is not mean or grouchy. And He's not mad at you either. Never forget that.

. . . .

God, You are the One who loves me forever! Thank You for Your amazing kindness to me, even when I don't deserve it. Thanks for gently showing me when I mess up and helping me make better choices when I come to You.

GOD CREATED YOU FOR A PURPOSE

*We are His work. He has made us to belong
to Christ Jesus so we can work for Him.
He planned that we should do this.*
EPHESIANS 2:10

You are God's very own masterpiece. Did you know that? You are a work of art. God smiles when He looks at you. You were created in His own image. God created you for a purpose—to love Him and to love others.

He has certain things that He specifically created you to do during your time here on earth. He gave you gifts and abilities that are special and unique. The things that you enjoy doing aren't a coincidence. God can use them in your life in powerful ways. Thank Him for making you just the way you are.

God, You are my Creator, and You made me the way I look and with the personality I have to do good works for You. I'm thankful for the gifts and talents You gave me. Help me use them in ways that honor You. Help me to get better at my talents as I grow up so that I can be ready to use them as You want me to.

THE BEST GIFT OF ALL

Men become right with God by putting their trust in Jesus Christ. God will accept men if they come this way. All men are the same to God. For all men have sinned and have missed the shining-greatness of God. Anyone can be made right with God by the free gift of His loving-favor. It is Jesus Christ Who bought them with His blood and made them free from their sins.
ROMANS 3:22–24

God is so kind and good that He sent Jesus to show us how much He loves us. Jesus took all of our sin and shame on Himself and set us free. We are right with God because of Jesus and His great gift! When someone gives us a special gift, we write them a thank-you note, right? Spend a few minutes writing God a thank-you note for His great gift.

....

God, Your kindness makes my heart so happy. I don't understand how You did something like this or why; I just know You did it because You love me, and I'm truly thankful. Thank You for the very best gift of all.

A FAITH-THING

*You have closed me in from behind and in front.
And You have laid Your hand upon me. All You know is
too great for me. It is too much for me to understand.*
PSALM 139:5–6

How is it possible for God to know me personally? How
can He know my name and care about the things I care
about? With billions of people to watch over, it seems
completely impossible! How can I be special to God?

Our human minds can't understand this kind of
thing. The Bible says that such knowledge is too much
for us to grasp. We can't possibly understand everything about the Creator of all things. God is the God
of the impossible (Luke 1:37).

The truth is, He does know you. He does care. He
loves you beyond what your mind can fully understand.
He just does. It's a faith thing. Ephesians 3:20 tells us
that God is able to do exceedingly, abundantly more
than what we could ever ask or even think! Caring
about us personally is one of those things.

....

*God, help me to trust what Your Word tells me about You.
You are able to do more than I could ever imagine.*

If someone has the gift of speaking words of comfort and help, he should speak. If someone has the gift of sharing what he has, he should give from a willing heart. If someone has the gift of leading other people, he should lead them. If someone has the gift of showing kindness to others, he should be happy as he does it.
ROMANS 12:8

No matter where you are or what kind of personality you have, God is calling you to be a leader in certain situations. If you tend to be quiet and shy, God can use you to lead with a gentle strength. If you are outgoing and extroverted, God can use your spirit of enthusiasm to share His love with many. The point is to allow God to use the personality He's given you in the way that He wants to.

As you pray, offer your personality up to God to be used in the best possible way. Thank Him for giving you exactly what He wanted you to have.

Lord, please give me the courage to lead well when You ask me to, in school, at church, or at home.

GOD SEES IT ALL

Do not let anyone pay back for the bad
he received. But look for ways to do good
to each other and to all people.
1 THESSALONIANS 5:15

Have you ever been accused of something you didn't do? Maybe your brother or sister blamed you for something or someone said you lied when you didn't? Stuff like that happens. . .and it hurts. You wish that God would speak up—right out of the sky—and tell the other person what really happened!

But God promises that He sees and that He will take care of things in the best way possible. It can be so hard to be nice to someone who isn't telling the truth about you. But God says to leave the paybacks to Him (Romans 12:19). He's the only One who sees every side of the story. Pray for the truth to come out, and pray for the person who hurt you. They need help from Jesus too.

....

God, I know how much You love me, and I know
You've seen everything that has happened. Help me
let go of bad situations like this so I don't carry around
anger in my heart. Help me to trust You more.

MAKING MESSES

Trust in the Lord with all your heart, and do not trust in your own understanding. Agree with Him in all your ways, and He will make your paths straight.
PROVERBS 3:5–6

Have you ever gotten yourself in a big mess and then tried to fix it all on your own? Sometimes we get mixed up in things that we aren't supposed to. Can you think of a time when this has happened?

God wants us to come to Him before and during our plans. He wants you to get in the habit of talking to Him about your plans before you do something. But even if you've made a bad choice and taken a wrong path, you are never on your own. God has promised to never leave you!

When you realize you're stuck in a mess, stop right then and talk to Jesus about it. Ask Him to help you get back on the path that was meant for you. God is faithful even when you make a mess of things.

God, I've made a mess, and I need some help. Please lead me back on the right path and help me come to You first before I decide to do things.

MUSTARD SEEDS

*Jesus said to them, "Because you have so little faith.
For sure, I tell you, if you have faith as a mustard seed,
you will say to this mountain, 'Move from here to over there,'
and it would move over. You will be able to do anything."*
MATTHEW 17:20

The next time you're in the grocery store, go look for the mustard seeds in the spice section. Or ask your parents if you have any at home. They are super tiny, aren't they? God says that even if you have faith that small— He will show up in BIG ways!

It's never about the size of your faith—it's about the power of God. Faith is all about putting your trust in a big God. You can trust that when you are weak, He is strong. And as you grow up and get used to taking your eyes off problems and looking for God to show up instead, your faith will grow and grow.

. . . .

*God, sometimes my faith is pretty small. Please show
me that You are working in my life in big ways.
Help my faith to grow as I begin to trust You.*

DOING A GOOD JOB

"His owner said to him, 'You have done well.
You are a good and faithful servant. You have
been faithful over a few things. I will put many
things in your care. Come and share my joy.' "
MATTHEW 25:21

God has given each of us special jobs to do while we're here on earth. What are your gifts and talents? Think about them. God wants you to use them for a purpose. It's no accident that you are good at certain things and not so good at others.

Wouldn't it be a great feeling for God to tell you that you're doing a great job with what He's given you? And when you show that you are faithful (you've done a good job at some things), God will give you more and more things to be in charge of.

Sometimes people have trouble finishing a job well when they get bored or if the task gets too hard. But you can finish the job well because God is with you, always ready to help you along the way.

* *

God, thanks for the jobs You've given me.
Help me to be faithful and finish well.

LIVING IN THE MOMENT

But as for me, I trust in You, O Lord. I say,
"You are my God." My times are in Your hands.
PSALM 31:14–15

Kids are really good at living in the moment. Most children don't have trouble worrying about the future or what they're going to do with their lives. They are happy to do what's right in front of them and then simply move on to the next thing. That's probably one of the reasons that Jesus is often telling grown-ups to be more like children!

But as you grow up, it's really easy to start worrying about the future. Ask God to help you stay childlike when it comes to worry. Get in the habit of saying, "I trust You, God. My times are in Your hands." Then picture God holding your whole life in His strong hands. Trusting God like that makes all of your problems seem so much smaller.

. . . .

God, thank You for my life. I trust You with it. I know
You're holding me in Your hands. Please help me to
continue living in the moment with You as I grow up.

GOD KNOWS ME

O Lord, You have looked through me and have known me. You know when I sit down and when I get up. You understand my thoughts from far away. You look over my path and my lying down. You know all my ways very well. Even before I speak a word, O Lord, You know it all.
PSALM 139:1–4

Any time you start to wonder if God cares about you, read Psalm 139! God knows every single thing about you. He even knows your thoughts. And before you say a word, He knows what it will be. He knows when you're going to sit down, stand up, go to school, think a thought—everything!

Even if you've ignored God every day before now, He hasn't ignored you. Open your Bible and read the rest of Psalm 139. Even though there are billions of people in this world, God made you and He cares about you. He knows your name. He loves you more than you could ever imagine.

God, will You open up my heart so that I can be fully aware of You? I want to see You at work in my life and truly believe how much You love me.

COURAGE TO DO THE RIGHT THING

Open your mouth for those who cannot speak,
and for the rights of those who are left without help.
PROVERBS 31:8

You probably know by now what a bully is. It's important to have conversations with your parents and other trusted grown-ups in your life about what to do when you come in contact with a bully.

God cares about people who are bullied and put down by others. He tells those of us who are strong to stand up for those who are too weak or small or scared to stand up for themselves. If you know someone who is being hurt by someone else and doesn't have the strength to get help, go tell someone you trust who has the power to do something about it. like a parent or a teacher.

Pray for God to give you the courage to do the right thing. Ask Him to comfort the hurting person and that justice (fair treatment) would happen for everyone involved.

. . . .

Lord, please give me courage to stand up for what
is right and good. Fill my heart with kindness for
people who are being bullied. Show me how to help.

GOD IS PRESENT

*How great is Your loving-kindness! You have stored
it up for those who fear You. You show it to those
who trust in You in front of the sons of men.*
PSALM 31:19

When you trust God, He becomes a very present help
in times of trouble (Psalm 46:1)! A very present help.
Think about that for a minute: God is very present. . .He
is with you this very moment as you read these words.
His power and comfort are constantly available to
you. He is good, and He wants to show His goodness to
you on a daily basis.

When you focus on all the bad things and worry
about stuff that hasn't even happened yet, you forget
about God. But when you focus on God and talk to Him
instead of worrying, He actually shows Himself to you
in each moment.

We may live in a broken world—but we have great
hope! Because He is with us. . .our times are in His
hands. . .and His perfect plan is trustworthy!

....

*God, thank You for being with me in each
moment. Forgive me for the times I worry.
Please replace my worries with Your peace.*

SEEING GOD

No person has ever seen God at any time. If we love each other, God lives in us. His love is made perfect in us. He has given us His Spirit. This is how we live by His help and He lives in us.
1 JOHN 4:12–13

One day, we'll be able to see Jesus again face-to-face. That's the promise we have as God's children. But for now, the Bible tells us that we see God by seeing His Spirit alive and at work in us and in believers around us. God is love. And when you see love in action, you are seeing God at work.

We also see evidence of God in all of His creation. God can speak to us in so many ways. He is the Master Artist. He paints us a new picture with every sunrise and sunset. Do you see God at work around you? Name some ways that you have seen God this week.

....

Thank You for Your amazing creation that speaks to me every day, God! Help me love others well so that they can see You at work in me.

GIFTS THAT PLEASE GOD

*Remember to do good and help each
other. Gifts like this please God.*
HEBREWS 13:16

Do you know what your love language is? A love language is the way that someone feels and experiences love. Researchers have narrowed them down to several main ways that people feel loved: acts of service (like doing chores for your mom), gift giving, quality time, physical touch (hugs!), and words that make them feel good about themselves. It's important to know what your love language is so that you can share it with the people you love. And it's important that you know the love language of the special people in your life so that you can find ways to show them how loved they are.

The Bible says that one of the ways that God feels our love is when we make good choices and help each other. He loves it when we help others feel loved too. What ways can you show love to God and others this week? Can you make some homemade gifts? Can you write a note to someone with an encouraging message? Ask God to give you some great ideas.

*God, please help me to show You and
others how much I love them.*

BUILDING ON THE ROCK

"Whoever hears these words of Mine and does them, will be like a wise man who built his house on rock. The rain came down. The water came up. The wind blew and hit the house. The house did not fall because it was built on rock. Whoever hears these words of Mine and does not do them, will be like a foolish man who built his house on sand. The rain came down. The water came up. The wind blew and hit the house. The house fell and broke apart."
MATTHEW 7:24–27

Do you have a basement in your home? Some homes are built on a concrete slab or a crawl space. Every home needs a solid foundation, or it will collapse.

Jesus talked about this truth too. He said that having a strong faith in Jesus is just like building your house on the rock. When storms or the bad things in life come your way, you won't get knocked down because your hope is in Jesus. Are you building your house on the Rock?

．．

Lord, I want to build my life upon the truth of Your Word. You are my Rock that will get me through the storms of life.

"First of all, look for the holy nation of God. Be right with Him. All these other things will be given to you also."
MATTHEW 6:33

In Matthew 6:25–34, Jesus was telling His followers a simple story that they could understand about birds and flowers. He wanted them to understand that if they trusted God, they didn't need to worry. Jesus wants us to know the same thing.

Birds and flowers don't worry, because God takes care of them. He gives birds food to eat, and the flowers were created to look beautiful. God says not to worry because He knows that we need to have clothes and that we need to eat. He promises to provide for our needs.

The New Living Translation of the Bible says it this way: "Seek the Kingdom of God above all else, and live righteously, and he will give you everything you need." When you seek God's kingdom first, He'll make sure you have exactly what you need at exactly the right time. Just like the birds and the flowers.

. . . .

Jesus, thank You for using birds and flowers to teach me not to worry. Help me remember that every time I see them.

GIFTS THAT HELP

*God has given each of you a gift. Use it to help
each other. This will show God's loving-favor.
If a man preaches, let him do it with God speaking
through him. If a man helps others, let him do it
with the strength God gives. So in all things God may
be honored through Jesus Christ. Shining-greatness
and power belong to Him forever. Let it be so.*
1 PETER 4:10–11

Have you ever taken music or art lessons? Or do you
practice extra hard at basketball or soccer? It's good
to work at getting better at the talents God has given
you. He wants to use your talents so that God can show
His love and shining-greatness to others through your
special gifts.

How can you use your gifts and talents to help others? Can you help someone who is struggling in an area
that you're really good at? Can you make a special picture for someone who is sick or having a hard time? Ask
God to show you some special ways that you can use
your gifts to help others and show God's love.

· ·

*God, please show me ways that I can use my
gifts to help others and spread Your love.*

AMAZING LOVE

Christ became human flesh and lived among us.
We saw His shining-greatness. This greatness is
given only to a much-loved Son from His Father.
He was full of loving-favor and truth.
JOHN 1:14

God could have chosen a million different ways to save us, but He chose to show us the true meaning of love. "Greater love has no one than this: to lay down one's life for one's friends" (John 15:13 NIV). Giving up your life for someone else is true, unselfish love.

God chose to send His Son into the world to live just like us, to become our friend. . .and to eventually lay down His life and die on the cross to show how much He truly loves us. Jesus knew it would hurt. He knew He would suffer. He knew He would be betrayed by some of His best friends. But He did it all anyway so that we could be made right with God—once and for all. His unfailing love is available to all of us who seek Him!

God, Your amazing love for me is something I'll always
be trying to figure out. Thank You for sending Jesus
to make me right with You. I love You, Lord!

GET YOUR LIFE FROM JESUS

"Get your life from Me and I will live in you. No branch can give fruit by itself. It has to get life from the vine. You are able to give fruit only when you have life from Me. I am the Vine and you are the branches. Get your life from Me. Then I will live in you and you will give much fruit. You can do nothing without Me."
JOHN 15:4–5

Jesus loved telling powerful stories by using simple, everyday things that people could understand. . .like grapes. Have you ever seen a grapevine? Sure you have! When you bring grapes home from the store, the fresh, juicy grapes are still attached to the vine. The grapes that have fallen off at the bottom of the bag are usually squishy and gross. That's because they aren't connected to the vine anymore.

Jesus says that He is our Vine and we are like the branches. We get our freshness and life from Jesus! If we try to live our life without Him, we'll end up like those squishy grapes at the bottom of the bag.

. . . .

Jesus, show me how to stay close to You and get true life from You.

He who goes about talking to hurt people makes secrets known. So do not be with those who talk about others.
PROVERBS 20:19

No one likes to be made fun of. The words we say to other people are very important to God. The things we talk about and the jokes we laugh at tell others who we really are on the inside.

Do you know what gossip is? It's when you make fun of or talk bad about others behind their back. Gossip hurts. But the truth is, it's easy to gossip when everyone else is doing it. It can sneak up on you when you are least expecting it. Even at church!

Gossip is no laughing matter. God takes it very seriously. It hurts others, it ruins friendship, and it is never harmless.

If you're in a group and someone starts to gossip, try to change the conversation to something else. If that doesn't work, simply walk away. Ask God for help to do the right thing.

....

God, please forgive me for the times I've gossiped about other people. I know gossip is hurtful, and I'm sorry. Please help me to watch my words.

BEING TRUTHFUL

*"These are the things you are to do: Speak
the truth to one another. Judge with truth
so there will be peace within your gates."*
ZECHARIAH 8:16

Do your parents, friends, and family members trust you? Trust is a big deal. When people trust you, you have a good relationship. Parents are willing to give you more privileges, rewards, and responsibilities when they trust you. Friends are glad to have you in their lives. Family members are happy to have you around when you are trustworthy.

The opposite is also true. Lying breaks a relationship. You lose trust, privileges, and rewards when you lie. It takes a long time to build trust back up even after one lie. Little lies and big lies are all the same in God's eyes. But God can help! Ask Him to help you think before you speak and to keep you from being tempted to lie. The consequences of lying are always worse than whatever you are trying to cover up in the first place.

....

*God, please forgive me for the times I haven't told
the truth. Help me to be a trustworthy person
and to build trust back up in my relationships.*

You will lead me by telling me what I should do.
And after this, You will bring me into shining-greatness.
PSALM 73:24

Moment by moment, God is with you and available to guide you through any and every situation. He wants to speak to you. He wants to share your joy during times of blessing. He wants to comfort you during times of pain and sadness. And He wants to guide you through times of confusion and decision-making.

Isaiah 30:21 (NIV) says: "Whether you turn to the right or to the left, your ears will hear a voice behind you, saying, 'This is the way; walk in it.'"

Remember that when you gave your life to Christ, the Holy Spirit miraculously came to live inside of you and you are no longer alone! You don't have to figure things out by yourself anymore.

God will guide you as you listen for Him and He always makes Himself clear. If there is something He really wants you to do or to know, you will hear it again and again. . .through His Word, through a song, through someone at church. . . Be listening!

....

Thanks for leading me as I listen for Your voice, Lord.

THE ARMOR OF GOD

This is the last thing I want to say: Be strong with the Lord's strength. Put on the things God gives you to fight with. Then you will not fall into the traps of the devil.
EPHESIANS 6:10–11

Open your Bible to Ephesians 6:10–17. Can you pick out all of the special equipment that God gives His children? Draw a picture of the armor and mark all the special pieces. Can you picture Jesus putting this armor on you?

The belt of truth keeps everything in the right place. When you know the truth about who God is and who He says you are, you can make it through any battle. Add your breastplate, the shoes of peace, the shield of faith, the helmet of salvation, and the sword of the Spirit. You are dressed to keep the faith in a messy world. Post your picture on the wall to remind yourself to put your armor on every day.

. . . .

Thank You, Lord, for giving me Your armor of protection. You've thought of everything I will need. Please show me how to use every tool the right way.

Christ was before all things.
All things are held together by Him.
COLOSSIANS 1:17

Jesus holds the whole world together. He is more powerful than anything you can imagine, and yet, He loves and cares for you. He knows everything about you, and He cares about the things you're going through. Sometimes that can be hard to believe, but the Bible tells us it is true. And Jesus will show up and be very real in your life if you let Him. Have you invited Him in?

Jesus wants you to talk to Him about everything. Is there a problem you are facing that feels too big or too small for God? Talk to Him about it. Tell Him how you really feel. Ask Him to help you believe that He cares about every little thing. Every big thing too.

The closer you get to Jesus, the more your thoughts begin to match up with Jesus' thoughts. And your problems become a whole lot smaller as you experience God's greatness.

....

Lord, I'm so amazed that You truly care so much for me.
I want to get closer and closer to You every day.

LAMPS AND LIGHT

*Your Word is a lamp to my feet and a light to my
path. . . . The opening up of Your Word gives light.
It gives understanding to the child-like.*
PSALM 119:105, 130

Flashlights are fun to use at night. Do you have one in your room? It's so cool to push a button or flip a switch and the darkness turns to light. That same thing can happen when you read God's Word, the Bible.

When you open the Word of God and start understanding God's truth for your life, it's like a switch flips in your heart. Suddenly, you have God's plan for your life right in front of you. It helps you know what path to take.

A flashlight doesn't help you see everything around you. It gives just enough light to help you see where to go next. Just like the Bible. As you get to know God, He'll give you just enough information to take the next step. And as you keep coming back to Him for truth, He'll keep lighting up your path.

*Thank You for lighting up my path, Lord. I trust You to
show me the next step at just the right time.*

A DIVINE CREATION

Men cannot say they do not know about God. From the beginning of the world, men could see what God is like through the things He has made. This shows His power that lasts forever. It shows that He is God.
ROMANS 1:20

Sometimes it can be hard for grown-ups to believe in a God they can't see. Kids often have a much easier time believing. Why do you think that is? Talk to your parents about why this might be true.

The Bible tells us that if we take a look at creation all around us and see the amazing things He's made (including you and all the other humans around you!), no one can say that there isn't a God. It's pretty obvious that our beautiful world wasn't created by accident. *Divine* means that something is from God. There is divine order and beauty in everything that God made. Science is full of the evidence of God.

Thank God today for His beautiful creation. Thank Him for creating you and your family too.

....

God, Your creation is amazing and beautiful. Thanks for everything You've made.

CHOOSING HAPPY

I know how to get along with little and how to live when I have much. I have learned the secret of being happy at all times. If I am full of food and have all I need, I am happy. If I am hungry and need more, I am happy. I can do all things because Christ gives me the strength.
PHILIPPIANS 4:12–13

Did you know that happiness is a choice? A guy named Paul, who wrote the book of Philippians, said that he figured out the secret. Can you guess what it is? Look for clues in verse 13 above.

The secret is allowing Jesus Christ to be your source of strength and happiness no matter what. Do you feel content and happy with what you already have, or are you always wishing for the next thing? Ask God to help you choose happiness. Choosing to be thankful for what you have can change a grumpy, no-good day to a day full of happiness and adventure. You get to make this choice yourself, every single day.

Jesus, please change my attitude from always wanting more to being thankful for what I already have.

BUTTERFLIES AND TRANSFORMATION

*All of us, with no covering on our faces, show
the shining-greatness of the Lord as in a mirror.
All the time we are being changed to look like
Him, with more and more of His shining-greatness.
This change is from the Lord Who is the Spirit.*
2 CORINTHIANS 3:18

Have you ever seen a caterpillar transform into a butterfly? It's amazing to watch! The caterpillar has to stop eating, hang upside down, and spin itself into a chrysalis where the metamorphosis occurs before it can become a butterfly.

God transforms us kind of like that butterfly. As you get to know Jesus and allow His Spirit to begin speaking to you and leading you, you begin to transform and you start looking a lot more like Jesus. Not with your hair color or facial features, but your heart begins to look a lot more like the heart of God.

When you begin following Jesus, there is freedom and love and help for your transformation process as He prepares you to fly.

....

*Jesus, I want my heart to look like Your heart.
Thanks for the great work You're doing in me!*

PRAYING FOR FRIENDS AND FAMILY

"I will give them one heart, and put a new spirit within them. I will take the heart of stone out of their flesh and give them a heart of flesh."
EZEKIEL 11:19

Do you have some friends or family who don't know Jesus? Maybe they've had a lot of bad things happen to them or they just don't feel like they need God in their lives.

Make a list of at least five people you know who need the love of Jesus. Your prayers are powerful, and they can make a huge difference! Come back to this page as much as you can to pray for them.

Insert the name of all five of the friends and family members in this prayer:

Jesus, I pray for_____ today. I pray that they would see the evidence of You all around them today in Your creation and through the love of Your people. Please begin to soften their hearts of stone and give them a heart that seeks You. Help them know that no one loves them more than You do.

....

Lord, help my loved ones to see You through my love.

FOLLOWING JESUS

He said to the Jews who believed, "If you keep and obey My Word, then you are My followers for sure."
JOHN 8:31

Your parents really like it when you obey, right? They want you to obey to show them that you love them and trust them to know what's best for you. It's the same with Jesus. He doesn't want us to obey His words because He wants us all to act like robots. Nope, He wants a relationship with us where we love and trust Him. We obey Jesus because we trust that He loves us more than anything and wants the very best for our lives.

Have you ever read through Matthew, Mark, Luke, and John? These books of the Bible are called "the Gospels," and they teach us about the life and words of Jesus. If you start reading them, you will learn more about Jesus and what He has to say to you today. Just like the disciples, you can learn how to follow Jesus by knowing and trusting Him.

....

Thank You for showing me how to follow You, Jesus. I know You want the very best for me because You love me so much!

PERFECT PEACE

*"You will keep the man in perfect peace whose
mind is kept on You, because he trusts in You."*
ISAIAH 26:3

The Bible talks about taking every thought captive
(2 Corinthians 10:5). Do you know what that means
and why it is so very important? It means that whenever anything happens to you—good, bad, boring, you
name it—take it immediately to God in your mind. Talk
to Him about it. Perfect peace happens only in the
presence of God. It doesn't mean that nothing bad
will ever happen to you. But He will give you peace for
each moment that you share with Him.

Wouldn't it be great to live out your life in perfect
peace? Well. . .you can! If you're waiting at the dentist's
office bored or nervous, talk to God. If you are happy
or sad or mad or excited, talk to God. Share each moment with Him. He offers perfect peace in every
moment for anyone who fixes their thoughts on Him!

. . . .

*God, I really do want to live my life in perfect peace with
You. Please help me to remember You in all things and all
situations. Thank You that You are constantly with me!*

BIG PROMISES

"Ask, and what you are asking for will be given to you. Look, and what you are looking for you will find. Knock, and the door you are knocking on will be opened to you. Everyone who asks receives what he asks for. Everyone who looks finds what he is looking for. Everyone who knocks has the door opened to him."
MATTHEW 7:7–8

Jesus makes some really big promises to us. And the great thing about this is that Jesus always keeps His promises. He will never let you down. There are three really big promises in our verses for today.

He promises that if you ask, it will be given to you. Does this mean that everything you ask for will be yours? Not exactly. This means that anything you ask for that is part of God's will for your life, will be yours.

As the Holy Spirit changes your heart, you will begin asking for the things that God wants for you. He always says yes to those prayers! When you ask according to God's will, look for God in everything, and knock on the door of heaven. . .you will find everything you're looking for. That's a promise!

Jesus, thank You for always keeping Your promises.

THE GOLDEN RULE

"Do for other people whatever you would like to have them do for you. This is what the Jewish Law and the early preachers said."
MATTHEW 7:12

You've probably heard of the Golden Rule before, right? Know what it means? It's asking yourself this question before doing something to someone else: *Would I be happy if someone did this to me?*

Jesus says that this rule pretty much sums up every other rule. It's about love. *Is what I'm about to do the loving thing to do?* If not, the best idea is to not do it. If you go ahead and do it anyway, you can expect some consequences. That's just the way life works. Our actions always show if we are loving and following Jesus. And our actions always speak louder than our words. And Jesus can help you to act in loving ways even when you don't feel like it.

Imagine what the world would be like if everyone followed the Golden Rule! Why not start right there in your family?

....

Jesus, please help me to think about my actions before I do something that isn't loving. I want to show by what I do that I'm Your follower.

IT'S GREAT TO BE DIFFERENT

Do not act like the sinful people of the world. Let God change your life. First of all, let Him give you a new mind. Then you will know what God wants you to do. And the things you do will be good and pleasing and perfect.
ROMANS 12:2

God made you different on purpose. It's great to be different. Kids who aren't following Jesus spend a lot of their time and energy trying to fit in. But that's not at all what Jesus wants. He wants you to be uniquely you. You have a unique fingerprint and a unique personality. Even identical twins have different fingerprints. That's because you were made to be different and you are special to God.

If you catch yourself getting worried about fitting in, don't stress about it. Just ask Jesus for help. He knows what you struggle with. He can help you make the right choices about friends and fitting in. He wants to give you a new mind that will help you want God's will for you.

....

Lord, thanks for making me different. Help me not care so much about what other people think. I want to be the me You created me to be.

ASK GOD FOR WISDOM

If you do not have wisdom, ask God for it.
He is always ready to give it to you and
will never say you are wrong for asking.
JAMES 1:5

New followers of Jesus need wisdom. And all you have to do is ask for it! Jake had some math problems that didn't make any sense. He was stuck and getting very discouraged. Jake was reminded of his dad though. Jake's dad works in a high-tech environment, and some of the problems he deals with every day are very technical and complicated. So guess what he does? He asks God for help with his job.

God has all the answers to absolutely everything. He is happy to help and give us wisdom. So Jake prayed and asked God to help his brain understand the math problem, and he was able to understand and move on to the next question. You can come to God with any question or problem you have. Get in the habit of asking God for help in everything.

....

Thanks for giving me wisdom, God. You have
all the answers. Remind me that You are here
for me in every problem and situation.

IMPORTANT WORDS

*Speak with them in such a way they will want to
listen to you. Do not let your talk sound foolish.
Know how to give the right answer to anyone.*
COLOSSIANS 4:6

We've talked about how important our words are
to God. God wants us to speak truthfully and lovingly
to others (Ephesians 4:15). He wants everything about
our lives to be based on His love. . .especially our
conversations!

Over and over in the Bible, God talks to us about
our words:

- Be quick to listen and slow to speak (James 1:19).
- People will give an account for every careless
  word they speak (Matthew 12:36).
- Those who consider themselves religious and
  yet do not keep a tight rein on their tongues deceive themselves, and their religion is worthless
  (James 1:26).

These are just a few! Our words are so important. Ask
God to help you with your words.

· ·

*God, please help me to bring all of my words to
You, first, before I say them to someone else.
I want to honor You with my words and bring
hope and love to people by the things I say.*

MESS-UPS

*If we tell Him our sins, He is faithful and we
can depend on Him to forgive us of our sins.
He will make our lives clean from all sin.*
1 JOHN 1:9

Nobody is perfect except Jesus, and we all make mistakes because we're human. Some people forget God for a while until they realize how much they've messed up without Him. But He never forgets you.

When you've messed up big, talk to Jesus. Turn back to God and start to trust Him again. . .to really trust Him. God is faithful. That means He always keeps His promises and He will never leave you. . .even if you mess up big.

There is something very powerful about coming to God and confessing your sins to Him. He already knows what you've done, but He wants to talk with you about it anyway. He wants to help you through it and give you peace. He wants to remind you who you really are to Him.

He will give you the power to trust Him more and to make better choices next time.

. . . .

*God, I know I've messed up big. Will You please forgive
me and change my heart? Show me a better way.*

GOD'S WILL FOR YOU

Be full of joy all the time. Never stop praying.
In everything give thanks. This is what God
wants you to do because of Christ Jesus.
1 THESSALONIANS 5:16–18

You've heard people talk about "God's will" before, right? Why worry about what God wants you to do when you can simply talk to God about it and listen for His answer?

Sometimes God's will is very clear. Like it is here in 1 Thessalonians. God clearly says what He wants you to do: Be joyful. Pray always. Give thanks in everything. Those are three very clear statements of God's will for you.

You might look at this and think, *How could I possibly be full of joy all the time? How can I never stop praying? How can I be thankful all the time?* Well, the Bible answers those questions too. You can't do it on your own. It's only by the power of Jesus working in you.

As you commit your life to Jesus, you'll begin to see joy and thankfulness bubbling up inside you as you become more and more like Him.

....

I commit to following Your will for my life, Jesus.
Thank You for being clear with me.

WALKING WITH GOD

For You have set my soul free from death.
You have kept my feet from falling, so I
may walk with God in the light of life.
PSALM 56:13

Do you like going on walks with your family? God wants you to take a walk with Him that never ends. Walking with God is having a relationship with your Creator. It is knowing Him, loving Him, trusting Him, and worshipping Him in each moment. The Bible promises that we can walk in God's presence each and every moment.

What does that look like? Walking with God is not just reading a Bible verse each morning and checking God off your list for the day. It's knowing that He is with you in every moment and inviting Him to be a part of your daily life. It's letting Him be a part of every conversation you have, every thought you think, and everything you do. Can you picture yourself on a never-ending walk with Jesus? Where is He leading you?

. . . .

Jesus, I invite You to hold my hand and walk
with me every day. I'm excited for this
lifelong adventure with You.

Jesus said, "Come!" Peter got out of the boat and walked on the water to Jesus. But when he saw the strong wind, he was afraid. He began to go down in the water. He cried out, "Lord, save me!"
MATTHEW 14:29–30

Jesus loves a good adventure. In fact, one time He called His friend Peter to get out of their boat and walk on top of the water. Can you imagine that? Peter jumped right in and thought it was really cool. But then He took His eyes off Jesus and started looking around. What do you think happened next?

Yep, Peter realized what he was actually doing, and he got scared. Then he started to sink! What does this true story tell you? It's easy to get scared really quick when you take your eyes off Jesus.

You'll probably have some scary things happen to you as you grow up. But you don't have to live in fear. Here's what Jesus has to say to you: "Don't be afraid. . . . Take courage. I am here!" (Matthew 14:27 NLT). Keep your eyes on Jesus, and you're in for a great adventure.

....

Help me to always keep my eyes on You, Jesus.

CONVERSATIONS WITH GOD

*I cried to the Lord in my trouble, and He
answered me and put me in a good place.*
PSALM 118:5

Having a friendship with God is just like having a relationship with one of your good friends. Sometimes you talk and your friend listens. Then sometimes your friend talks and you listen. It wouldn't be a very good friendship if your friend was the only one talking and you always had to do the listening, right?

When we talk to God, He wants to have a real conversation with us. Praying is not about sending a wish list to heaven. It's telling God how you feel about certain things and then listening for His answer.

God answers us in lots of ways. He can speak to us through just about anything (one time He even spoke through a donkey! Look up the story here: Numbers 22:28–30). He loves to speak through His Word, through worship songs, through the love of another Jesus follower, through His creation. . .but God's ways are limitless.

The next time you pray, sit and listen for God to answer. What is He telling you?

. . . .

*Thanks for talking to me, Lord. Help me
to hear and understand Your answers.*

Jesus said to him, " 'You must love the Lord your God with all your heart and with all your soul and with all your mind.' This is the first and greatest of the Laws. The second is like it, 'You must love your neighbor as you love yourself.' All the Laws and the writings of the early preachers depend on these two most important Laws."
MATTHEW 22:37–40

God made His purpose to His followers pretty clear (and that includes His purpose for *you* too!): He wants us to love Him and love others. That sums up *everything* the Bible is trying to teach us. If we're just following rules, we've missed the whole point.

Remember, God *is* love. Everything He does is done from a foundation of love. That's what He wants from us too. He wants us to obey because of love, to serve Him because of love, to worship Him because of love, to be kind to our neighbors because of love. The only way we can do any of that is because He loved us first (1 John 4:19).

....

Thank You for making my purpose easy to understand, Jesus. I love You. I'll do my best to love others too—with Your help!

Christian brothers, live your lives as I have lived mine.
Watch those who live as I have taught you to live.
PHILIPPIANS 3:17

Do you have good people to look up to in your life? It's important to have people in your life who are older and can encourage you in your walk with God. The role models God wants us to look up to are the ones who love God and love others well. They build their lives on the foundation of God's truth, and they've seen Him work in their lives for many years.

Who can you go to and ask for prayer when you're facing something difficult? Who can help you grow closer to Jesus? Do you have parents, grandparents, teachers, or older friends who love Jesus? Take some time and think about these things. Ask Jesus to bring these kinds of people into your life. If you already have them, be sure to thank them. Write them a note and tell them how much you appreciate the difference they are making in your life.

God, thanks for putting great people
in my life. Please give me wisdom
about who I look up to as I get older.

MADE ON PURPOSE

We do not compare ourselves with those who think they are good. They compare themselves with themselves. They decide what they think is good or bad and compare themselves with those ideas. They are foolish.
2 CORINTHIANS 10:12

God doesn't want us to compare ourselves with others. Wanna know why? Because when you compare yourself to others, you either start to feel prideful (like you're better than others), or you get very insecure (like you're not as good as others). But God made you unique on purpose.

You are awesome just the way you are. It's who you are on the inside that matters to God. He made you on purpose for a purpose. The way you look and the gifts and talents you have can all be used by God. He has great plans for your life.

So, if you wish your hair was a different color or your body was bigger or smaller, talk to God about this. Ask Him to show you what you look like to Him. Ask Him to help you trust that you were made this way for a purpose.

....

God, please forgive me for comparing myself to others. Help me to be content just the way You made me.

BE LIKE JESUS

"But love those who hate you. Do good to them. Let them use your things and do not expect something back. Your reward will be much. You will be the children of the Most High. He is kind to those who are not thankful and to those who are full of sin."
Luke 6:35

You might not have many enemies yet, but there will be a lot of people you come across in your lifetime who don't like Christians. People who are angry at Christians have usually been wounded deeply by other people pretending to be Christians. They think that God is just like the Christians who have hurt them. They've believed a lie about God. Knowing and remembering this can help us love them even when they don't act very lovable.

This is true for many kids who act mean too. Mean kids have usually been deeply hurt by someone else. They are acting out of what they've seen. If you know a few mean kids, ask Jesus to help you show kindness to them.

Jesus, help me to see others like You see them. Help me to be kind to people who are unkind so that they can know what You are really like.

JUST BE YOU

*Everything God made is good. We should not put anything
aside if we can take it and thank God for it.*
1 TIMOTHY 4:4

God created you, and everything He created is good!
So just be the person God created you to be. You might
wish you were more outgoing like some of your friends
or that you looked a little different. . .but God created
you exactly the way He wanted you to be.

Your personality is the way God made you, and He
wants to use that for His glory. He gave you the body
you have for a reason. . .so take good care of it and
thank Him for it.

Ask God to change your heart to match His desire
for you. God looks at you and sees a work of art. Ask
Him to give you that same attitude about yourself—
not so you'll be prideful or full of yourself, but so you
will respect and enjoy the body and personality God
gave you!

. . . .

*God, please change my heart to match Yours.
Help me to believe that what You say is true.
Help me to be myself—just the way You made me.*

A HUGE PROMISE

Do not worry. Learn to pray about everything. Give thanks to God as you ask Him for what you need. The peace of God is much greater than the human mind can understand. This peace will keep your hearts and minds through Christ Jesus.
PHILIPPIANS 4:6–7

God tells us that instead of worrying about anything, we should simply pray!

When you hold worries inside of you, they can actually hurt your body. Stress can cause a lot of health problems. God wants you to bring those fears and worries to Him instead. He promises that when you do that, a very powerful thing happens: He'll give you His peace.

This peace is special; it's a peace that happens no matter how difficult the problem is that you are facing. It's a peace that doesn't really make sense to anyone else but you and God. He wants you to be thankful instead of stressed, and He alone can help you do that. He'll also guard and protect your heart and your mind. What a huge promise!

. . . .

God, I pray for Your peace to wash over me as I bring my worries to You. Thank You for always keeping Your promises.

CHOOSING LIFE

"I call heaven and earth to speak against you today. I have put in front of you life and death, the good and the curse. So choose life so you and your children after you may live. Love the Lord your God and obey His voice. Hold on to Him. For He is your life, and by Him your days will be long."
DEUTERONOMY 30:19–20

Life with Jesus is the most amazing adventure you can ever go on. The Bible says that eternal life is knowing God through His Son, Jesus Christ (John 17:3) and that Jesus came to give us abundant life (John 10:10)—even here, right now on this earth. . .you don't have to wait for heaven to experience this abundant life adventure. It starts now!

You'll have a choice every day of your life. To follow Jesus and stay close to Him. Or not. Choosing Jesus won't always be easy. Some days it will be downright hard. But it is always worth it. What will you choose?

Thank You for giving me life, Jesus. Help me stay close to You all the days of my life.

GENTLE WORDS

A gentle answer turns away anger,
but a sharp word causes anger.
PROVERBS 15:1

Have you ever been in an argument with a sibling or a friend? Both of you want to be right about whatever is happening. And you want to make sure that the other person knows that you are right.

But you have a choice to make in that moment: Do you want to be happy. . .or right? Instead of stirring up someone else's anger, Jesus tells us to answer with gentleness. If you answer someone with gentleness, it can turn off that person's anger and then the argument is over. And if that doesn't work. . .you can just walk away until you both have calmed down.

Proverbs 29:11 (ESV) says, "A fool gives full vent to his spirit, but a wise man quietly holds it back." Ask Jesus to help you with your anger. Go to Him first before getting in an argument.

. . . .

God, help me to be strong and gentle at the
same time. Please give me Your strength as I
face anyone who may be angry in the future.
Help me to answer gently or to walk away.

STRONG AND BRAVE

"Have I not told you? Be strong and have strength of heart! Do not be afraid or lose faith. For the Lord your God is with you anywhere you go."
JOSHUA 1:9

We're going to remind you of this over and over: If you've trusted Christ as your Savior, the Spirit of God Himself is alive and well and working inside you at all times. What an astounding miracle! The Creator of the universe dwells within you and is available to encourage you and help you make good choices in every moment.

Be encouraged! Even when it might feel like it, you are truly never alone. You always have access to God's power. God wants you to be strong and brave, relying on His power.

The issue that has your stomach in knots right now? Ask the Lord to go before you. The problem that makes you wish you could hide under the covers and sleep until it's all over? Trust that God Himself will never leave you and that He is working everything out.

Lord, help me to be strong and brave, knowing that my courage and strength comes from You.

GOD IS AWAKE

My help comes from the Lord, Who made heaven and earth.
He will not let your feet go out from under you. He Who
watches over you will not sleep. Listen, He Who watches
over Israel will not close his eyes or sleep. The Lord watches
over you. The Lord is your safe cover at your right hand.
PSALM 121:2–5

Did you know that God doesn't ever go to sleep? When
you lay your head down at night, you can know for sure
that God hears your prayers before bed, and He will
watch over you all night long. You never have to be
afraid!

Victor Hugo, a famous author from the 1800s,
said, "Have courage for the great sorrows of life and
patience for the small ones; and when you have labor-
iously accomplished your daily task, go to sleep in
peace. God is awake."

There are some big words in there, but the point
is to have courage and patience as you go throughout your days. And then when you lay your head down
to sleep, you can do so peacefully because God is in
control. He is awake, and He's watching over you.

God, thank You for always watching over me.

*"I do not call you servants that I own anymore.
A servant does not know what his owner is
doing. I call you friends, because I have told
you everything I have heard from My Father."*
JOHN 15:15

Because of all that Jesus did for you on the cross, He gave you complete access to God! But you're not only His child, He calls you His friend too! How amazing is that?

Have you ever thought about what being friends with Jesus means? When you look for a friend, you want to find someone who is kind, trustworthy, and willing to listen. Jesus wants to have that very same kind of relationship with you. He wants to have conversations with you. He wants to be there for you every day.

God wants you to live a life of confidence and joy, knowing that you are never alone and trusting that God is working everything out for your good and His glory—even the bad things that happen during this life. When trouble comes your way, you can look at it with peace knowing that your very best friend has it covered.

·····

*Jesus, I'm so amazed that You call me Your friend!
Thanks for always looking out for me.*

WILLING TO SHARE

*Each man should give as he has decided in his heart.
He should not give, wishing he could keep it. Or he
should not give if he feels he has to give. God loves a
man who gives because he wants to give. God can give
you all you need. He will give you more than enough.
You will have everything you need for yourselves. And you
will have enough left over to give when there is a need.*
2 Corinthians 9:7–8

You may have a little. . .or you may have a lot. But even if you don't have much to share, you can bless someone with whatever you do have.

Jake and Jessa sponsor a needy child in a poor country. They love it when he sends them drawings and pictures. They helped him buy a new bed so that he would have a place to sleep. Many kids around the world don't have as much as most Americans have. So be thankful for all that God has blessed you with and always be willing to share.

. . . .

*God, thanks for all of my blessings. Show me
ways that I can share them with others.*

GOD'S LOVE

For I know that nothing can keep us from the love of God. Death cannot! Life cannot! Angels cannot! Leaders cannot! Any other power cannot! Hard things now or in the future cannot! The world above or the world below cannot! Any other living thing cannot keep us away from the love of God which is ours through Christ Jesus our Lord.
ROMANS 8:38–39

God promises that nothing can separate us from His love when we've decided to follow Jesus. That's a very important thing to know! Nothing you could do could make God love you more or less than He does right now.

We all mess up and make big mistakes sometimes. That doesn't change how much God loves you. Sometimes we sacrifice and do great things for God. That doesn't change how much God loves you either. His love isn't normal. You can't do anything to earn it or change it. It just is.

Ask God to open your heart to believe this truth. Then share it with everyone you know.

....

Thank You for loving me more than I can imagine, God. Help me to share Your love with everyone around me.

TELLING THE TRUTH

A lying tongue hates those it crushes, and a mouth that speaks false words destroys.
PROVERBS 26:28

Telling the truth is a really big deal to Jesus. That's because telling a lie causes all kinds of trouble. Even if you tell one little lie about something unimportant, people can get hurt. They learn that you can't be trusted. Earning trust back from a parent, family member, or friend after you've lied is a really hard thing to do.

The Bible tells us that a liar crushes other people's spirits. But gentle words that are true can be healing and life giving. Remember, words are very powerful! Once said, you can never really take them back. . .even if you want to. You can use words for good or for evil. So go out of your way to bring kind and truthful words to people you usually don't talk to. Greet people with a smile and an encouraging word. Ask God to use your words to bring people life today.

God, please help me to be very careful with my words and to always tell the truth. Use my words to bring other people life and joy.

GODLY LIGHT

We have this light from God in our human
bodies. This shows that the power is
from God. It is not from ourselves.
2 Corinthians 4:7

An amazing thing happens when we choose to follow Jesus: His Spirit comes to live inside of us to light up our lives. Do you have any candles decorating your house? They might be nice to look at on their own, but when you light them with a match or a lighter, the fire makes them become powerful, producing light and heat. That's kinda how it is with God's Spirit in us. You probably have natural ability to do a lot of things on your own, but with God's power you can do so much more!

So when your feelings are hurt. . .or sad things happen. . .or you don't feel like you can do something on your own, you can rely on the power of God that is alive in you. You don't have to depend on yourself.

....

Lord, please remind me that You are alive in me.
I want this life to be about Your love shining through
me and not about me and what I can do on my own.

NOBODY IS PERFECT

Live and work without pride. Be gentle
and kind. Do not be hard on others.
Let love keep you from doing that.
EPHESIANS 4:2

You can probably think of at least one person who really bothers you. Maybe there's a mean kid at school or a bully down the street. Have you ever thought about why they act the way they do? Maybe they aren't getting their needs met from their parents and they are trying to get attention and affection from anyone else they can.

There is always a reason for why people act the way they do, even if they don't know it themselves. But God knows! That's why you should pray for the people who bother you. God knows exactly why they act the way they do, and your prayers can help change their heart—and yours in the process! Nobody is perfect, and even your best friend will act in ways that bother you at some time or another. Have lots of grace for that because of God's love living inside you. Be patient and gentle with others.

....

God, I don't always understand why people act the way they do, but I pray You would help me love them anyway.

*Trust in the Lord, and do good. So you will live in the
land and will be fed. Be happy in the Lord. And He will
give you the desires of your heart. Give your way over
to the Lord. Trust in Him also. And He will do it.*
PSALM 37:3–5

It's easy to look at this verse and think, *Hey, if I'm
happy to be a Christian, God will give me everything I
want!* But when we really start to happily follow Jesus,
God changes our hearts so completely that all we ever
want is what He wants. When you commit everything
you do to God, you will begin to see the desires of
your heart start to match God's desires.

How can you be happy in the Lord? Start your
morning with thankfulness. Ask God to bless your day
and for opportunities to be a blessing to everyone
around you. Talk to God about each plan, issue, and
problem you face. Thank Him for big and little blessings that come your way.

....

*Lord, I commit my whole heart to You—
and all of my plans and ideas. Thank You for
Your blessings and Your great love for me.*

GOD GOES BEFORE YOU

"The Lord is the One Who goes before you. He will be with you. He will be faithful to you and will not leave you alone. Do not be afraid or troubled."
DEUTERONOMY 31:8

Have you ever jumped off the diving board into a big pool? It seems a little bit easier if you're not the first one to try it, right? It feels better if you let someone else go first and see that they aren't scared and won't get hurt. And it gives you the courage to try it for yourself.

The Bible says that God goes before you just like that. He says that you don't have to be afraid because He already knows what's ahead for you. He'll always jump off the diving board first just so you won't be scared. He is with you and will never leave you alone. He offers you courage every step of the way.

So relax and enjoy the amazing adventure that God has prepared just for you.

....

Thanks for always going first, Lord. You love me so well. Thanks for never leaving me alone. I'm excited for all the things You have planned for my life.

BEYOND YOUR IMAGINATION

God is able to do much more than we ask
or think through His power working in us.
EPHESIANS 3:20

The New International Version of the Bible says that God can do "immeasurably more" than what you could imagine. When God's power is at work within you, the possibilities are beyond your imagination.

Whatever problem you are facing right now—big or small—God cares. As you pray and think about it, don't put God in a box thinking that there's no way out or that there is only one right answer. His response just might be beyond your understanding and your wildest imagination.

Remember that things aren't always what they seem. If you feel disappointed in God's answers to your prayers, look outside the box. God is always, always working everything out for your good (Romans 8:28). God sees all. What may have felt like the best answer may have been very bad for you or someone you love. Trust that God can do much, much more than anything you could ever ask or imagine!

....

Lord, help me to trust that You are working
everything out in the best possible way.

IN JESUS' NAME I PRAY

So when the name of Jesus is spoken,
everyone in heaven and on earth and
under the earth will bow down before Him.
PHILIPPIANS 2:10

The Bible tells us that the name of Jesus is very powerful. That's why many Christians end their prayers with "In Jesus' name." Some of the most powerful prayers are simply: "Jesus!" In those quick moments when that is all you can think to pray, you are putting your trust in the power of Jesus and asking for His help and protection.

Saying the name of Jesus is not a magical word that will have power on its own. People use the name of Jesus all the time without even a thought toward Him. (The Bible calls that taking God's name in vain; that's why saying things like "OMG" isn't such a great idea.) When you call on Jesus' name in prayer, you put your hope and trust in Jesus Himself who holds all the power.

Is there some fear you're dealing with? Call on the name of Jesus for help.

Jesus, I trust that Your power is unlimited.
Please come to my rescue.

THOUGHTS AND FEELINGS

Jesus knew what they were thinking. He said,
"Why do you think bad thoughts in your hearts?"
MATTHEW 9:4

The things you think about are important to Jesus. That's because your thoughts affect everything you do and say.

Check out this verse in Ephesians 4:31: "Put out of your life all these things: bad feelings about other people, anger, temper, loud talk, bad talk which hurts other people, and bad feelings which hurt other people."

God wants His followers to stop hurting each other and having bad thoughts. But you can't do this on your own. You need supernatural help from the Holy Spirit. Philippians 4:8 tells us what to think about instead! Open your Bible to check it out or see page 122. This is part of "taking your thoughts captive" like we've talked about too.

God wants to help you become more like Him, and He is able to work miracles in your life today. He is always ready to help you stop thinking bad thoughts and turn your attention to Him instead.

···

Lord, I want to think good things about You and
other people. Please help me become more like You.

I pray that you will know how great His power is for those who have put their trust in Him. It is the same power that raised Christ from the dead. This same power put Christ at God's right side in heaven.
EPHESIANS 1:19–20

How does your family celebrate Easter? Easter eggs and springtime activities are a fun way to celebrate that God makes all things new. . .but do you know the real reason behind Easter? Easter is the celebration that Jesus is alive! We are remembering when Jesus rose up from the grave on the third day after He died for our sins on the cross.

Jesus is still alive today! And when He went back to heaven, He sent His very Spirit to continue living inside of our hearts. Jesus is getting everything ready for us in His Father's house (John 14:2), and soon He will come back for all of us who love Him.

Until then, His powerful Spirit is alive right inside of us. And we can celebrate that He is alive every single day.

Thank You for Easter, Jesus. Remind me to celebrate that You are alive every day!

HEARING FROM JESUS

Long ago God spoke to our early fathers in many different ways. He spoke through the early preachers. But in these last days He has spoken to us through His Son. God gave His Son everything. It was by His Son that God made the world.
HEBREWS 1:1–2

Through Jesus, God created and saved the world. Jesus is God in a perfect human body. When you look at Jesus, you get a clear picture of God. And He can speak directly to you. When you pray, make it a conversation where you talk a little and then listen a little.

You may not hear an out-loud voice, but Jesus can speak to your heart as He answers your prayers and talks to you. And He will make Himself clear to you if you seek Him. In Jeremiah 29:13 (NIV), God says, "You will seek me and find me when you seek me with all your heart."

Ask Jesus to speak clearly to you today. What is He saying?

. . . .

Jesus, thanks for wanting to talk to me!
Help me to be able to hear from You
and get to know Your voice.

LEARNING HIS VOICE

> *"My sheep hear My voice and I know them. They follow Me. I give them life that lasts forever. They will never be punished. No one is able to take them out of My hand."*
> JOHN 10:27–28

Jesus wants you to know His voice just like sheep know their shepherd's voice. In sheepherding countries, sheep from different flocks may get together to graze, but they can easily be divided back into their own herd simply by following their master's voice.

As you begin learning how to hear God's voice, you'll continue to see that when God speaks to you, it will always line up with His words in the Bible. If you are not sure if something is from your imagination or if it is from God, simply ask God to be clear to you. Remember that if there is something God really wants you to do or to know, you will hear it again and again. . . through His Word, through a song, through someone at church. . .if you're listening!

Jesus, please open my ears to get to know Your voice. I want to follow You with all of my heart.

GOD'S KIND OF CLOTHES

*Therefore, as God's chosen people, holy and
dearly loved, clothe yourselves with compassion,
kindness, humility, gentleness and patience.*
COLOSSIANS 3:12 NIV

Jessa loves fashion. She enjoys choosing outfits and finding pretty accessories to match. She says that fashion is half her life! While we laugh with her about that, we know that God says there are much more important things for us to "wear" each day.

Look at today's verse. What does it say that God wants us to clothe ourselves with? God's kind of clothes are made of love: love for God and love for others. That's what really matters!

Wrapping yourself up in compassion, kindness, and patience will warm you and everyone around you too! God loves you so much, and He wants you to share His love with other people. Picking out nice clothes is fun, but putting on God's clothes is the first step. So the next time you're headed out, reach for God's kind of clothes and you'll be ready for anything.

. . . .

*God, help me to wear things that make a difference in
other people's lives like love, compassion, and kindness.
Thanks for loving me and showing me Your truth.*

HE KNOWS YOU BY NAME

*The Lord said to Moses, "I will do what
you have said. For you have found favor in
My eyes, and I have known you by name."*
EXODUS 33:17

How cool that the God who made the earth and every-thing in it—the stars, the mountains, the ocean. . . everything—knows you personally! God knows your name and everything about you. He loves you just the way you are. And He set you on earth at this exact time in history for a purpose.

God wants you to know Him. He wants you to know how much He loves you and tenderly cares for you. He also wants you to choose to love Him back. . . and to love others through Him.

God promises to go with you wherever you go. He wants to be your best friend and to teach you His ways.

Have you told God how much you love Him today? He is waiting to hear from you.

. . . .

*Lord, it's sometimes hard to believe that You
know everything about me and love me anyway.
But Your Word tells me it's true. I love You, God.
Thanks for always being here for me!*

EQUAL IN GOD'S EYES

Then Peter said, "I can see, for sure, that God
does not respect one person more than another.
He is pleased with any man in any nation
who honors Him and does what is right."
ACTS 10:34–35

You are just important to God as your pastor, your principal. . .or even the president! The Bible says that God doesn't play favorites (Galatians 3:28). That means that He doesn't think one person is more important than another person because of what he or she does or because of where they live or how much money they have. That kind of stuff doesn't matter to God.

We are all equal because of Jesus. A wise person said that the closer we get to Jesus, the more equal we become. That's because God's love changes our hearts to be more like His. God's door is wide open for everyone no matter what kind of job they do or what kind of family they come from. The love of Jesus is for everyone!

....

God, thank You that Your door is open to everyone!
You love each of us abundantly and equally.

GOD IS WITH YOU

Yes, even if I walk through the valley of the shadow of death, I will not be afraid of anything, because You are with me. You have a walking stick with which to guide and one with which to help. These comfort me.
PSALM 23:4

God has promised to be with you through everything. God has the tools you need for every job and the map you need for every journey. If He asks you to go somewhere or do something, He'll always provide exactly what you need at the right time. And you can count on Him to keep His promises.

Look at what Psalm 139:7–10 (NIV) says: "Where can I go from your Spirit? Where can I flee from your presence? If I go up to the heavens, you are there; if I make my bed in the depths, you are there. If I rise on the wings of the dawn, if I settle on the far side of the sea, even there your hand will guide me, your right hand will hold me fast."

No matter where you go, God is with you!

. . . .

Father, thank You for being with me and providing everything I need. I trust in Your promises.

STRENGTH FOR THE WEAK

He gives strength to the weak. And He gives power to him who has little strength. Even very young men get tired and become weak and strong young men trip and fall. But they who wait upon the Lord will get new strength. They will rise up with wings like eagles. They will run and not get tired. They will walk and not become weak.
ISAIAH 40:29–31

Could you use a large helping of God's power in your life? Who couldn't? The Bible says that those who wait for the Lord—the people who pray—will gain new strength!

God gives strength and power to people who feel like they don't have any. . .if we simply come to Him in prayer and wait expectantly. Waiting for the Lord in prayer means that you expect Him to show up and keep His promises. You look for Him and you put your hope in Him.

Have you ever gone to God and prayed for strength before? Do you know some family members or friends who could use God's strength? Pray for them.

. . . .

Thank You for giving us Your strength, God.
I pray for my family members who need You too.

GENTLE AND RESPECTFUL

Your heart should be holy and set apart for the Lord God.
Always be ready to tell everyone who asks you why you
believe as you do. Be gentle as you speak and show respect.
Keep your heart telling you that you have done what is right.
If men speak against you, they will be ashamed when they
see the good way you have lived as a Christian.
1 PETER 3:15–16

If you love God and treat other people with kindness, people are going to wonder what makes you different. They may even ask you questions about why you act the way you do.

Some people will disagree with your faith in unkind ways. But before you get angry, ask for God's help. He is right there with you, and He sees everything that's happening. He wants you to answer with gentleness and respect, not anger and embarrassment.

The reason people ask is because they are looking for hope too! And they want to know if yours is real or not!

. . . .

God, help me remember that everyone else is looking for
hope in You too. You created them that way. Help me be
gentle and respect others when I share my faith in You.

He will feed His flock like a shepherd. He will gather the lambs in His arms and carry them close to His heart. He will be gentle in leading those that are with young.
ISAIAH 40:11

Jesus is your gentle Shepherd. Can you picture Him carrying you close to His heart? You are so important to Him, and He loves you so much.

Psalm 23:1–3 says, "The Lord is my Shepherd. I will have everything I need. He lets me rest in fields of green grass. He leads me beside the quiet waters. He makes me strong again. He leads me in the way of living right with Himself which brings honor to His name."

Commit to staying close to your Shepherd, Jesus. He will always lead you on the right path. He will refresh and restore your life, making you strong. Pray that Jesus continues to make His voice known to you.

....

Jesus, thank You for caring for me like a gentle shepherd. I love the thought of You carrying me close to Your heart. I will follow You, Jesus. Help me to recognize You as You speak to me.

YOU GET WHAT YOU PLANT

Do not be fooled. You cannot fool God.
A man will get back whatever he plants!
GALATIANS 6:7

We're going to talk about gardening for the next few days. Jake and Jessa love to help plant things and make seed markers every year. Have you ever planted a garden? You probably know that whatever kind of seed you put in the ground is the kind of plant that will grow. How silly it would be if you planted peas but pumpkins grew instead!

In the Bible, this is called sowing and reaping. You get back whatever you plant. This is true in the garden of our hearts too. If you plant thankfulness and generosity in your heart, you'll grow blessings. What do you think a person would grow if they planted lies and anger in their hearts? There are rewards for sowing good things and consequences for sowing evil.

Are you planting good things or harmful things in the garden of your heart? Ask Jesus to help you. . . . He is really good at gardening!

....

Lord, I want good things to grow in my heart,
so I'm going to need Your help. Will You help
me plant thankfulness and generosity?

THE FRUIT OF THE SPIRIT

But the fruit that comes from having the Holy Spirit in our lives is: love, joy, peace, not giving up, being kind, being good, having faith, being gentle, and being the boss over our own desires. The Law is not against these things.
GALATIANS 5:22–23

When Jesus Christ is firmly planted in your heart, the fruit of the Spirit begins to grow. . .and that's a really big deal! As the Spirit of God works in the garden of your heart, He produces spiritual fruit because of what Jesus did for you on the cross. His death and eternal life give you new life. . .just like a spring garden. This special fruit is love, joy, peace, patience, kindness, goodness, faithfulness, gentleness, and self-control.

As you continue to follow Jesus, this fruit begins to take root and grow in your heart. . .getting bigger and bigger until you are bursting with spiritual fruit. So much so that everyone around you will know that it is God who did the gardening in your heart.

···

God, please fill me up with the fruit of Your Spirit. I want to burst with this special fruit.

GROWING MORE FRUIT

And this is my prayer: I pray that your love will grow more and more. I pray that you will have better understanding and be wise in all things. . . . And I pray that you will be filled with the fruits of right living. These come from Jesus Christ, with honor and thanks to God.
PHILIPPIANS 1:9, 11

Have you seen a garden that is overgrown with weeds? The weeds take over and hog all of the water and nutrients that the good plants need to grow. The good plants end up dying or producing very little fruit.

Selfishness can be a weed in the garden of your heart. If you plant selfishness, it can take over and harm the good fruit of the Spirit that God has planted in your heart.

Don't forget, though, that Jesus is a really good gardener. He knows what to do with all the weeds. If you have weeds of selfishness growing, ask Jesus for help. He can get rid of all the weeds and help you grow more healthy fruit instead.

Jesus, please remove any weeds that are growing in my heart. Make good fruit grow instead.

THE GREAT EXCHANGE

He answered me, "I am all you need. I give you My loving-favor. My power works best in weak people." I am happy to be weak and have troubles so I can have Christ's power in me. . . . For when I am weak, then I am strong.
2 Corinthians 12:9–10

Have you ever taken a pair of pants that didn't fit back to the store and exchanged them for a different size or for something else altogether? Did you know that God likes to exchange things too? He's often exchanging old for new, death for life, ashes for beauty, sadness for joy, despair for praise (see Isaiah 61:3). And He also exchanges our weakness for His strength.

Do you need God to exchange something for you? What do you need to bring to Him that you would like replaced with something that only He can give? Self-ishness for spiritual fruit? Sadness for joy? Weakness for strength?

Bring all of your weaknesses to Jesus and lay them at His throne. Ask for Him to exchange your weaknesses for His power.

....

God, I'm so thankful that You exchange my weaknesses for Your strength.

A GOOD EXAMPLE

*Let no one show little respect for you because
you are young. Show other Christians how to live
by your life. They should be able to follow you in
the way you talk and in what you do. Show them
how to live in faith and in love and in holy living.*
1 TIMOTHY 4:12

When God's Spirit comes and lives inside of you, He gives you, His kid, the power to be an example to others. . .even to older people. Sometimes it takes the faith of a child to get a hardened heart to hear from God. You never know when your life will touch someone else's, but you can be sure that everyone you know is watching to see if your faith is making a difference in your life.

Even if there are other people you may run into who try their best to put you down. . .never forget that you are a child of the King and He is the One who determines your value. So keep your chin up and be a good example.

*God, thank You for showing me who I am in You!
Help me to be a good example to others!*

BEING SURE

Now faith is being sure we will get what we hope for.
It is being sure of what we cannot see.
HEBREWS 11:1

There was a dad in the Bible who needed help with his son. His boy had struggled with a major problem since he was born. The disciples tried to help, but they couldn't do anything, so the dad took the boy to Jesus. This dad had some doubts. He wanted to believe Jesus could do anything, but He wasn't quite sure yet. The dad said to Jesus, "I do believe; help me overcome my unbelief!" (Mark 9:24 NIV).

Did Jesus heal the boy and increase the dad's faith? Yep!

Faith is believing in the unseen. It's trusting that God is real and that He is alive and working in our lives. Sometimes kids have a much easier time trusting God than adults do. Why do you think that is? Talk about this with your parents.

. . . .

God, I want my faith in You to be strong. Forgive me for the times I've believed that I have to do things all by myself. Please help my unbelief and increase my faith.

BLESSED TO BELIEVE

He said to Thomas, "Put your finger into My hands.
Put your hand into My side. Do not doubt, believe!"
JOHN 20:27

Thomas was one of Jesus' original twelve disciples. He was with Jesus during His ministry on earth and yet still had a hard time believing that Jesus rose from the dead. Even after he saw the many miracles of Jesus with his own eyes! But Jesus knew that Thomas needed to see His scars for him to believe, so He showed them to Thomas up close.

When Jesus allowed Thomas to touch Him, He said, "Have you believed because you have seen me? Blessed are those who have not seen and yet have believed" (verse 29, ESV). Sometimes we wish we could see Jesus face-to-face just like Thomas. But did you catch what Jesus said to Thomas? "Blessed are those who have not seen and yet have believed." Jesus was talking about you and me! He said we are blessed because we have faith without actually seeing Him with our own eyes.

God, please keep growing my faith in You
as I wait to see You face-to-face one day.

THE FOUR SOILS

*"But those which fell on good ground have heard
the Word. They keep it in a good and true heart
and they keep on giving good grain."*
LUKE 8:15

Have you ever read the story of the soils? Jesus tells a parable in Luke 8 about a farmer who went out to plant seeds. Some seed fell on the path, some on the rock, some on thorns and some fell on good soil. The only seed that grew into a big crop was the seed that fell on good soil.

Jesus explained this parable to His followers so they would know what He meant. The seed that produced the good crop stood for people who heard God's Word and followed Him no matter what. They patiently trusted God for all things, and God blessed them for it. Read the rest of Luke 8 and learn about the other kinds of soil. Which one are you?

....

God, I want to be like the seed that fell on the good soil. Please make my heart open to hear Your Word and to put it into practice. I pray that You will bless my life and let me be a blessing to others.

THE BEST HIDING PLACE

You are my hiding place. You keep me safe from trouble.
All around me are your songs of being made free.
PSALM 32:7

Have you ever felt like hiding for a while? Maybe someone really hurt your feelings or you just don't feel like being around anyone. Everyone wants to hide sometimes.

One of the great things about being a child of God is that He offers to be a hiding place for you. Whenever you feel like you want to run from your problems, you can run to Jesus instead. He promises to help calm you down, and the Bible even says He sings over you (Zephaniah 3:17).

So the next time you feel like hiding, why not ask a grown-up to help you turn on some worship music and take a good time-out in your room? Talk to Jesus and listen to Him sing over you. He is the very best hiding place.

. . . .

Jesus, thank You for being a safe place for me to hide.
Help me turn my focus to You instead of to my problems.

DIFFERENT IS GOOD

It is true, we live in a body of flesh. But we do not fight like people of the world. We do not use those things to fight with that the world uses. We use the things God gives to fight with and they have power. Those things God gives to fight with destroy the strong-places of the devil.
2 CORINTHIANS 10:3–4

As a child of God, remember that you have spiritual armor (see page 47 and Ephesians 6:10–17). These are the weapons God has given you to protect you from being sucked in by the thoughts and actions of this world.

Ask God for help to live in this world but not be of it (John 17:14–16). This means that we don't have the same value system as the people of the world who aren't following Jesus. We're supposed to be different! Being different is good. Pray and ask God for the courage to be different. Picture yourself putting on the whole armor of God every day.

God, I'm so thankful for the spiritual armor You have given me. Strengthen me and train me to use my armor well. Please give me the courage to be different as I follow You.

GOOD AND FAIR CHOICES

O man, He has told you what is good. What does
the Lord ask of you but to do what is fair and to love
kindness, and to walk without pride with your God?
MICAH 6:8

In the Old Testament book of Micah, the people of Israel continued to disobey God. They were making really bad choices. . .even building altars to false gods! But God was still kind and patient with them. He used a prophet named Micah to remind them of what He wanted them to do.

Micah spoke to the people and told them that God wanted them to be fair in all of their ways, to be kind to each other, and to walk humbly with God without being prideful and selfish.

God is good, and all His ways are good. And He wants us to follow Him by making those same kinds of choices. How are you doing at being fair, kind, and humble? Are you walking with God each day. . .or choosing your own way?

··

God, please help me to walk closely with You each day.
Help me to be fair and kind, just like You are!

FAITHFUL IN THE BIG AND SMALL

*"He that is faithful with little things is faithful
with big things also. He that is not honest with
little things is not honest with big things."*
LUKE 16:10

If you asked your friend to feed your fish while you went away on vacation and you came home to find your fish happy and well fed, you just might be willing to let that same friend watch your hamster too. And then maybe even your dog, right?

That's kind of like what Jesus is saying in this verse. If someone is faithful in the little things, they'll also be faithful in the big things. But if your friend forgot to feed your fish for a day or two, she'd probably forget to feed your dog too. If she wasn't trustworthy with something small. . .she probably won't be trustworthy with something big.

It's the same with us of course. If God gives you something small to do and you do it well. . .He will trust you to do even greater things.

....

*God, I want to be faithful to You in all things—
big and small. Help me to be a trustworthy person.*

POWERFUL PRAYERS

*Tell your sins to each other. And pray for each other
so you may be healed. The prayer from the heart
of a man right with God has much power.*
JAMES 5:16

Prayer is very powerful. The Bible tells us so! Something mysterious happens when we pray. We can't see exactly what happens in the unseen world when we pray, but we do know that your prayers matter to God and they can accomplish a lot.

The New Living Translation says: "The earnest prayer of a righteous person has great power and produces wonderful results."

God's Word tells us to pray for others so that they can be healed and restored. This is not only talking about physical bodies being healed, but also the hearts and minds of people being healed and made whole.

Who do you need to pray for? Make a list of family members with illnesses or broken hearts. Talk to God about each one and ask for His blessings on their lives.

....

*Thank You that my prayers matter to You, God! I bring my
friends and family before You and ask that You would
do Your healing work in their hearts and bodies.*

SHINING LIKE A STAR

Be glad you can do the things you should be doing.
Do all things without arguing and talking about how
you wish you did not have to do them. In that way,
you can prove yourselves to be without blame. You are
God's children and no one can talk against you, even
in a sin-loving and sin-sick world. You are to shine
as lights among the sinful people of this world.
PHILIPPIANS 2:14–15

Seems like everyone wants to be a star these days, right? Even kids make silly videos on YouTube and they become famous. What's the big deal about being a star anyway? Sure, you get lots and lots of attention, and maybe make lots of money to buy whatever you want. But Jesus wants us to be a different kind of star.

You are a child of God, and He gives you all the attention you could ever want. His desire is for you to shine for Him like stars in the sky. If you live like that, you'll stand out for sure!

. . . .

God, help me live a different kind of life than everyone
else. Help me light up the world with Your love
instead of seeking attention from others.

HEAR AND OBEY

Obey the Word of God. If you hear only and do not act, you are only fooling yourself. Anyone who hears the Word of God and does not obey is like a man looking at his face in a mirror. After he sees himself and goes away, he forgets what he looks like.
JAMES 1:22–24

God has a good sense of humor. He created laughter, after all. Imagine looking at yourself in the mirror and then completely forgetting what you look like as soon as you walk away. How silly would that be? God likes to explain things to us in ways that we understand. He's the best teacher, and He uses funny things to get our attention sometimes.

He says that if you hear God's Word and don't do what it says, you're just like the person in the mirror who forgets what he looks like. Instead, God wants us to know His Word and let our actions match what we've heard from God.

Ask God for help in knowing and doing His Word.

Lord, please help me to be a good listener and to put into action everything that I hear from You.

SCREEN TIME

So be careful how you live. Live as men who are wise and not foolish. Make the best use of your time. These are sinful days. Do not be foolish. Understand what the Lord wants you to do.
EPHESIANS 5:15–17

Is there a chance you're wasting time on things God might not want you to be doing? Look around at any time of day and you see just about everyone looking at a screen. There are many benefits to technology and social media, but there are also a lot of negatives. Does God care about your screen time usage? You bet!

Screen time and video games can easily become an idol. An idol is anything that comes before God in your life or turns your attention away from Him. Using screens and having fun online is okay as long as you are making wise choices about what you're doing and how long you're doing it. Talk to God about it. Ask Him to help you be wise with your screen time.

. . . .

God, please help me not to put screen time ahead of You. I don't want it to be an idol that gets in the way of my relationship with You. Help me be wise online.

Keep awake! Watch at all times. The devil is working against you. He is walking around like a hungry lion with his mouth open. He is looking for someone to eat. Stand against him and be strong in your faith.
1 PETER 5:8–9

Even though the enemy knows he's already been defeated by Jesus, he's still trying his best to get into your head and discourage you so you won't be able to live well for Jesus. That's why Jesus wants you to stay alert. Don't fall for Satan's tricks because he is the father of lies (John 8:44).

James 4:7 (AMP) says: "So submit to [the authority of] God. Resist the devil [stand firm against him] and he will flee from you." You have power in the name of Jesus to get rid of any evil you come up against.

You don't have to be afraid, just alert. Don't focus on the fear of the enemy. Focus on Jesus and His power to fight your battles!

Lord, You have given me everything I need to live my life for You. Help me to stay alert and not fall for any of the enemy's tricks.

We want to see our teaching help you have a true love that comes from a pure heart. Such love comes from a heart that says we are not guilty and from a faith that does not pretend. But some have turned away from these things. They have turned to foolish talking.

1 TIMOTHY 1:5–6

People were missing the point of Paul's message about Jesus in the Bible. They were spending their time arguing and talking about things that don't matter. Paul's main goal as a missionary is stated here in verse 5: He teaches so that all believers will be filled with love from a pure heart, clear conscience, and real-life faith.

The Christian life, a life of following Jesus, is all about love from a pure heart. When it becomes more about rules and religion. . .that is not real faith in Jesus. God's hope for you as a kid is that you'll be filled with purity and love. Psalm 119:9 (NIV) says: "How can a young person stay on the path of purity? By living according to your word."

. . . .

God, thank You that Your purpose for me is love and purity. Please fill me with Your love and presence.

GIFTS AND GLORY

So put away all pride from yourselves.
You are standing under the powerful hand
of God. At the right time He will lift you up.
1 PETER 5:6

Are you awesome at basketball and other sports? Do you have a beautiful singing voice? Or maybe gymnastics is your thing. Whatever gifts and talents you have, it's okay to be confident in your skills and giftedness. God has given you those gifts for a purpose.

But God doesn't want you to be prideful about those gifts and abilities. Romans 12:3 (NLT) says: "Don't think you are better than you really are. Be honest in your evaluation of yourselves, measuring yourselves by the faith God has given us."

Your gifts can be used for God, to bring Him attention and glory, or they can be used to bring attention and glory to yourself. Which one will you choose? Here's the thing: People who brag about their talents usually don't have a lot of real friends. People who bring attention to Jesus have an inner joy that comes from loving Him. The choice is yours to make.

Lord, I'm thankful for the talents
You've given me. I commit them to You.
Let them bring You attention and glory.

FORGIVENESS

You must be kind to each other. Think of the other person. Forgive other people just as God forgave you because of Christ's death on the cross.
EPHESIANS 4:32

Jesus' death on the cross paid for all of our sins once and for all. We still ask forgiveness from God when we sin because sin gets in the way of our friendship with Him. When we come to Him and confess our sins (telling Him we're sorry about what we've done), our friendship gets fixed quickly.

God wants us to forgive others just as quickly because when we carry around unforgiveness, it keeps getting in the way of everything. Are there friends or family members who have hurt you recently? Ask God for help to forgive them. Have you hurt someone's feelings yourself? Go to them and tell them you're sorry. Write them a letter if you have trouble saying these kind of things out loud. Ask God for the courage to do the right thing.

Lord, help me to forgive Your way—quickly and completely. Thank You for Your death on the cross that paid for my sins forever.

SHARING AND STUFF

Tell them to do good and be rich in good works. They should give much to those in need and be ready to share.
1 TIMOTHY 6:18

This verse in the Message translation of the Bible really tells it like it is: "Tell those rich in this world's wealth to quit being so full of themselves and so obsessed with money, which is here today and gone tomorrow. Tell them to go after God, who piles on all the riches we could ever manage—to do good, to be rich in helping others, to be extravagantly generous. If they do that, they'll build a treasury that will last, gaining life that is truly life" (1 Timothy 6:17–19).

Having lots of money and getting more money is the number one priority on many people's list. What about yours? Do you find yourself wishing you had a lot more stuff than you do? Ask God to change your desires to match His. Ask Him to instill a healthy view of "things" and money in your heart, always willing to share with others.

....

God, please help me to be content with what I have and willing to share with others in need.

There is no fear in love. Perfect love puts fear out of our hearts. People have fear when they are afraid of being punished. The man who is afraid does not have perfect love. We love Him because He loved us first.
1 JOHN 4:18–19

God is not mad at you. He sees you through the love and sacrifice of Jesus. So you can always approach Him without fear!

Those who are afraid of God's punishment don't understand who they are in Christ. You don't have to work harder or be a better Christian to earn God's love. Nothing you could ever do or not do could make Him love you more than He does right now.

When you begin to believe who you are in Christ, it changes everything. You start living differently. You realize how deeply loved you are, and it sets you free. As Jesus pours His love and His Spirit into your life, it spills over into the lives of those around you.

. . . .

You loved me first, God. That's how I know what love is. You laid down Your life for me. There is no greater love than that. Let my life be a living example of what Your love looks like.

DEEP ROOTS

"Good will come to the man who trusts in the Lord, and whose hope is in the Lord. He will be like a tree planted by the water, that sends out its roots by the river. It will not be afraid when the heat comes but its leaves will be green. It will not be troubled in a dry year, or stop giving fruit."
JEREMIAH 17:7–8

A tree with deep roots won't fall over when the storms come. It's strongly attached to the ground. It grows deep and is able to find the water it needs to stay alive during a dry spell.

The Bible tells us that when we trust in God and put our hope in Him, we are just like a tree planted by the water that isn't afraid when dry times come along. We know that God is our source of life and peace no matter what happens to us.

How are your roots? Are you firmly planted in God's Word? Pray for God to grow and water your faith roots.

Lord, I pray that You would help my faith to grow really deep roots. Help me to put my hope and trust in You alone.

STRONGER ROOTS

Have your roots planted deep in Christ. Grow in Him. Get your strength from Him. Let Him make you strong in the faith as you have been taught. Your life should be full of thanks to Him.
COLOSSIANS 2:7

The Bible talks a lot about gardening and growing things because people can understand more about God by looking at His creation. Check out this verse from the New Living Translation: "I pray that from his glorious, unlimited resources he will empower you with inner strength through his Spirit. Then Christ will make his home in your hearts as you trust in him. Your roots will grow down into God's love and keep you strong" (Ephesians 3:16–17).

If you want God's favor and blessing on your life, trust in Him. Put your hope in Him and find your confidence in Him alone. Ask the Holy Spirit to help you remember these important scriptures as you pray for God to continue growing your roots.

....

Jesus, thank You for making Your home in my heart. I want Your blessing on my life. I pray that You would grow my faith deep into the roots of Your love. I want to build my life upon You and Your truth.

THE BETTER CHOICE

Jesus said to her, "Martha, Martha, you are worried and troubled about many things. Only a few things are important, even just one. Mary has chosen the good thing. It will not be taken away from her."
LUKE 10:41–42

Martha was cooking and serving Jesus and His followers. This was expected of women during this time period. But Mary was sitting at His feet, wanting to hear everything Jesus had to say.

Martha did what everyone else wanted her to do, but Mary wanted to be with Jesus. Martha got mad at Mary and even whined about it to Jesus. Jesus replied in love but also told Martha the truth. Mary made the better choice.

Mary's choice made her sister mad, and the other people there probably looked down on her too. It's hard to go against the norms and follow Jesus. Ask Jesus for courage to follow Him even when everyone else says you're making the wrong choice.

Lord, please give me the courage to follow You and do what my heart is telling me even when other people disagree. I want to choose You even when it's not the popular choice.

TROUBLING THOUGHTS

Keep your minds thinking about whatever is true, whatever is respected, whatever is right, whatever is pure, whatever can be loved, and whatever is well thought of. If there is anything good and worth giving thanks for, think about these things.
PHILIPPIANS 4:8

Our thoughts can get us in lots and lots of trouble. It's easy to get off track and think about things we shouldn't. . .even when we're praying! We start off thinking about something good; then we easily get distracted by other thoughts.

The next time you find yourself thinking about something that isn't right, ask Jesus to step right into your thoughts and change them! Just speak His name and ask Him to come to your rescue. He can change the direction of your thoughts and turn them into thoughts and actions that are pure and true and lovely.

The name of Jesus has all power in heaven and earth (Philippians 2:10), and just speaking His name can change the direction of your thoughts.

Jesus, Your name is powerful. I pray You will step in and change my thoughts to be pure and true when I'm distracted.

KEEPING YOUR WORD

"Let your yes be YES. Let your no be NO."
MATTHEW 5:37

Jesus was teaching a large crowd about being trustworthy. Being a trustworthy person is very important to Jesus. It means that you tell the truth and you do what you say you're going to do.

If you told mom that you would clean your room right after school, make sure you get it done right away. If you promised your sister you would play games with her, make sure you do what you said you would instead of tricking her.

This is also called "keeping your word." When you keep your word, people trust you and they feel like they can count on you.

Ephesians 4:25 (MSG) says: "What this adds up to, then, is this: no more lies, no more pretense. Tell your neighbor the truth. In Christ's body we're all connected to each other, after all. When you lie to others, you end up lying to yourself."

The more trustworthy you are, the more privileges and responsibilities you'll be given as you grow up!

....

Jesus, I want to be trustworthy.
Help me to always keep my word.

DON'T GIVE UP

*If a man does things to please the Holy Spirit, he will
have life that lasts forever. Do not let yourselves get
tired of doing good. If we do not give up, we will
get what is coming to us at the right time.*
GALATIANS 6:8–9

Jesus tells a story of a very persistent woman in Luke 18:1–8. When you have time, read that story in the Bible. *Persistent* means that she never gave up. And she was rewarded for her persistence.

Quitters give up because they've run out of their own strength. They have nothing left to give, so they give up in defeat. But for followers of Jesus, we depend on His strength. Remember that His power shines through in our weakness. Allow Him to be your strength. Invite Him to give you power through His Spirit that is alive in you.

Keep coming back to God every day in prayer. Be persistent. Don't give up.

. . . .

*Lord, just like the persistent woman, help me to
always pray and never give up. Thank You that
I don't have to depend on my own strength.
I'd much rather count on Yours instead.*

PEACE IN THE MIDST OF PROBLEMS

Let the peace of Christ have power over your hearts.
You were chosen as a part of His body. Always be
thankful. Let the teaching of Christ and His words
keep on living in you. These make your lives rich and full
of wisdom. Keep on teaching and helping each other.
Sing the Songs of David and the church songs and the
songs of heaven with hearts full of thanks to God.
COLOSSIANS 3:15–16

When you let peace have power over your heart, it means that you have an inner calm that comes from trusting Jesus. When problems come, and they will, you trust in Jesus and His power over anything.

When you get in the daily habit of praying and taking all of your problems, worries, and concerns to Jesus, you begin to experience the kind of peace that Jesus offers.

When you're dealing with stress or too many things that are going on at once, turn your focus to Jesus and others. Help someone else. Turn on the praise music. And thank God for His peace in your heart.

....

Lord, help me focus on You daily. . .to look at
You and Your power instead of my problems.

*He gives us everything we need for life and for
holy living. He gives it through His great power.*
2 PETER 1:3

Jake and Jessa had a miraculous "God-thing" happen
to them. When our family moved to a new area where
we didn't know many people, God sent one of His
favorite daughters to our house. (Of course we are all
God's favorite children, but this elderly lady loved to
say that!) She was close to God, and she told us that
God sent her to our home to love us.

She was only with us for one year before she went
to heaven. . .but during her last year on earth, she
loved us dearly with the love of Jesus. She was
"Grammy B" to Jake and Jessa, and she came to all
of their events and birthday parties.

Right before she died, she shared this verse with
us from 2 Peter 1:3 as a reminder that God would
always give us everything we need if we trust Him.

. . . .

*Jesus, I'm so blessed by Your great power.
I can't thank You enough for giving me absolutely
everything I need to be close to You in each moment.*

A CLEAN LIFE

If a man lives a clean life, he will be like a dish made of gold. He will be respected and set apart for good use by the owner of the house.
2 TIMOTHY 2:21

If you're getting ready to eat your morning cereal, you pull a spoon out of the silverware drawer and you expect it to be clean, right? It's ready for you to use it to fill your body with breakfast. This verse in 2 Timothy is kinda the same thing. If you're clean before God, you're ready for Him to use you!

He wants to use all of us to do great things, but only those who live clean lives are ready for anything that God wants to do with their lives. If you found a dirty spoon in the silverware drawer, would you still use it to eat your cereal? Ew. . .gross! Nope, you'd put it in the dishwasher and go look for a clean spoon, right? Ask God to help you stay pure so that He can use you in the very best ways.

....

God, please give me a clean heart. Help me to live a clean life so that You can use me.

Whatever work you do, do it with all your heart. Do it for the Lord and not for men. Remember that you will get your reward from the Lord. He will give you what you should receive. You are working for the Lord Christ.
COLOSSIANS 3:23–24

Did you know that even homework and chores can be an act of worship to God? God sees you as you clean your room and do your chores at home. He cares about everything you're doing. So whatever you are doing, work at it with all your heart.

How would you work differently if you had to hand your homework straight to Jesus? Ask Him for help in seeing that Jesus is the One you are actually serving as you do your chores or school work. Pray for Him to give you joy in serving and helping around the house (turning worship music on while you work always helps too!). When you realize you're actually serving and worshipping God as you work, you become a joy to your parents and teachers too.

. . . .

Lord, remind me about the big picture when I'm working so that I can give my very best for You.

STEADY AND STRONG

The Lord is not slow about keeping His promise as some people think. He is waiting for you. The Lord does not want any person to be punished forever. He wants all people to be sorry for their sins and turn from them.
2 PETER 3:9

The Bible tells us that Jesus is coming back for all of us who love Him so that we can be with Him forever.

James 5:7–8 (MSG) says: "Meanwhile, friends, wait patiently for the Master's Arrival. . . . Stay steady and strong. The Master could arrive at any time."

Many people wonder why Jesus hasn't come back already and removed all the bad things from this world. The Bible has an answer for that. God loves us so much, and He wants everyone to trust Him. So, He is patient. . .giving people more time than they deserve to make a choice for Christ.

While we wait for His return, God wants us to be steady and strong in our faith.

. . . .

God, please help me to be steady and strong as I wait for Your return. Help me share Your love with friends and family who need to know about You.

GOD OR GOOGLE?

But the wisdom that comes from heaven is first of all pure. Then it gives peace. It is gentle and willing to obey. It is full of loving-kindness and of doing good. It has no doubts and does not pretend to be something it is not.
JAMES 3:17

Lots of people head straight to Google whenever they have a question. But heavenly wisdom is hard to find there.

You might eventually find the answer you're looking for, but it will be mixed with thousands of other opinions, and you have to sift through a bunch of junk to find some truth.

Heavenly wisdom is rarely found online unless you're looking up God's Word on a Bible app. When you need wisdom, the Bible tells us that we can ask God for it and He'll give it to us. . .just because we asked Him (James 1:5)! You never have to sift through any creepy content to find wisdom from God. He will give you pure answers that bring peace and love.

. . . .

God, I definitely need lots of wisdom in this mixed-up world. Please give me the desire to come to You for the answers to all my questions.

THE KINGDOM OF GOD

The proud religious law-keepers asked when the holy nation of God would come. Jesus said to them, "The holy nation of God is not coming in such a way that can be seen with the eyes."
LUKE 17:20

The Pharisees were the people in the Bible who thought they knew everything better than Jesus and didn't believe in Him. They were always trying to trick Jesus and get Him in trouble. They asked Jesus when the kingdom of God would come. They did not realize that by Jesus coming, the kingdom of God was already here.

The kingdom of God begins in your heart the moment you start believing in Jesus. Yes, we are waiting for Jesus to return so that we can physically be with Him forever. And yes, there will be a day when Jesus makes all things new and destroys all evil forever. But we don't have to wait for heaven to be a part of God's kingdom. It's already begun.

Jesus, thank You for filling me with love and joy right now. I'm so thankful we're friends and that I get to experience Your love and joy for all eternity too.

For to us a Child will be born. To us a Son will be given.
And the rule of the nations will be on His shoulders. His
name will be called Wonderful, Teacher, Powerful God,
Father Who Lives Forever, Prince of Peace.
ISAIAH 9:6

Do you have a nickname? Parents often have loving nicknames for their kids like "sweet pea" or "lovebug" or "champ." Sometimes nicknames are just silly, but they can also tell you more about a person.

Jesus has lots of nicknames. The names of Jesus are powerful, and they help you to know more about who God is. God wants you to know that He offers everything your heart needs, and His nicknames help you understand that better.

His nicknames show that He is all-powerful, He has the perfect answer for every one of your questions, He is the best parent who never makes a mistake, and He offers peace to all who seek Him.

. . . .

Thanks for telling me more about Yourself, Jesus.
I'm thankful to know You better and to know that
You've made a way to take care of every need I have.

HELP AND HOPE

The Spirit of the Lord God is on me, because the Lord has chosen me to bring good news to poor people. He has sent me to heal those with a sad heart. He has sent me to tell those who are being held and those in prison that they can go free.

ISAIAH 61:1

Jesus came to heal people with hurting hearts and to set people free. He's not just talking about physical conditions like people who need healing from an illness or someone who is in jail. He's talking about people with broken hearts and those who are stuck in fear. Jesus came to bring hope to anyone who needed it.

Have you ever felt sad or hopeless? Do you know anyone with a broken heart? Jesus loves to comfort people. And He can use you to help comfort hurting people too. The smile of a child can do wonders for some people. Ask Jesus to show you how He can use you to bring hope to hurting people. He'll point you in the right direction and give you courage as you go.

Jesus, please show me how I can help hurting people. Please give me courage to help bring hope to others.

*He gave the right and the power to become children
of God to those who received Him. He gave this
to those who put their trust in His name.*
JOHN 1:12

When you receive Jesus as your Savior, you become a child of God. The Bible tells us that you become "born of God" (verse 13). When you are born as a baby, you come alive physically. When you are "born of God," you come alive spiritually.

The day you accepted Jesus as your Savior is your spiritual birthday. It's something fun and important to celebrate! If you don't know the exact day, ask your family to help you estimate so you can plan a celebration.

Did you know that becoming a child of God comes with lots of gifts called an inheritance (1 Peter 1:4)? Only God knows what all this includes, but it's true that Jesus is the High King and you are His child. He has some pretty great gifts planned for you!

....

Jesus, I'm so thankful I gave my life to You and became a child of God! Thank You for providing an inheritance for me that will never go away.

You have seen how many places I have gone.
Put my tears in Your bottle. Are they not in
Your book? Then those who hate me will turn
back when I call. I know that God is for me.
PSALM 56:8–9

God knows when you're sad. The Bible says that He actually counts your tears and puts them in a bottle. The guy who wrote the book of Psalms had a lot of people who didn't like him. He was often talking to God about this. Do you feel like there are kids who don't like you very much? That can definitely hurt your feelings. God cares about that. He wants you to come to Him and talk to Him about it. He can help.

When you're feeling left out or not good enough for the other kids, Jesus wants you to know that He knows exactly how you feel. He had friends who betrayed Him too. And when you come to Jesus, He will remind you who you are: a child of the King. So lift up your head; you matter to God.

....

Jesus, thank You for understanding all my feelings.
I bring them to You. Remind me who I am.

"Do not work for food that does not last. Work for food that lasts forever. The Son of Man will give you that kind of food. God the Father has shown He will do this."
JOHN 6:27

Jesus' followers saw Him multiply the loaves and fishes to feed thousands. Jesus had given them all a free meal, and they knew He could do it again. They were hungry so they went to find Him.

They weren't necessarily coming to hear what Jesus had to say. They wanted something for nothing. But Jesus called them out on it.

He told them not to come just so He could fill their stomach with food, but to come and listen so that their hearts will be filled with life. Jesus was talking about "spiritual food." Just like we need to eat every day to live and grow, we need to have Jesus and His Word in us every day so that we can live and grow spiritually. What are some ways that you can grow spiritually?

. . . .

Jesus, thank You for my daily food so that I can grow physically. Help me to be hungry for Your spiritual food too.

BELONGING TO GOD

But now the Lord Who made you, O Jacob,
and He Who made you, O Israel, says, "Do not
be afraid. For I have bought you and made you
free. I have called you by name. You are Mine!"
ISAIAH 43:1

Have you ever felt like you don't fit in or you don't belong? It's important that you know that you belong to God. He wants you to know that no matter where you are, you are His! He knows your name, He is with you, and you never have to be afraid in new places or situations.

When Jesus Himself tells you who you are, it changes everything. You are His beloved child. He paid the price for your freedom when He gave His life for you on the cross. You have direct access to the One who sees everything and knows everything. You can be confident in every situation.

. . . .

Thank You for making me Your child, Lord. I'm so thankful
that I'm never alone. Help me to be confident in the truth
that You are always with me. I'm free to live a happy
life knowing that I'm Your precious child.

*"You are of great worth in My eyes. You are honored
and I love you. I will give other men in your place.
I will trade other people for your life."*
ISAIAH 43:4

The Message translation of the Bible says it this way:
"Because I am GOD, your personal God, The Holy of
Israel, your Savior. I paid a huge price for you. . .
That's how much you mean to me! That's how much I
love you! I'd sell off the whole world to get you back,
trade the creation just for you."

Do you believe that God loves you this much? You
are of great worth to God. He would trade the whole
world to get you back! He is your own personal God,
with you always. How does that make you feel?

God wants your friends and family to know this
too. How does God want you to share this amazing
love with them? Talk to Him about this. Ask Him for
courage to share His love with others.

···

*Thank You for Your amazing love for me, God.
Please help me have the courage to love others
and to share with them where my love comes from.*

HONORING GOD WITH MY PERSONALITY

*For God did not give us a spirit of fear. He gave us
a spirit of power and of love and of a good mind.*
2 TIMOTHY 1:7

God has given each of us different personalities, and there is nothing wrong with the way that God made you! He made some of us outgoing; some of us are curious and love school, some are creative, and some of us are organized and neat. However He made you, He wants you to use that personality to honor Him.

And while some of us might not like getting up in front of people, we never ever have to be afraid of what other people might say or think about us. Only God's opinion of you really matters. And He has given us His Spirit, which lives inside of us. And that is a Spirit of power, love, and self-control.

If you are ever feeling extra shy about anything, remember whose Spirit you can depend on. Ask Him to show up in big ways. He always does!

....

*God, thank You for my personality. You designed
me to think and act a special way. Help me to
honor You with my thoughts and actions.*

"All whom My Father has given to Me will come to Me.
I will never turn away anyone who comes to Me."
JOHN 6:37

When You come to Jesus for the first time or the millionth time, you can be sure that His arms are open wide. Even if you've messed up, Jesus says He will never turn anyone away who comes to Him.

Romans 2:4 (NLT) tells us some very special things about God: "Don't you see how wonderfully kind, tolerant, and patient God is with you? Does this mean nothing to you? Can't you see that his kindness is intended to turn you from your sin?"

It's the kindness of God that leads us to Jesus, to have our sins forgiven. If you've made a big mistake, the best thing you can do is to go straight to Jesus and talk to Him about it. Jesus promises that He will not turn you away. He will tell you He loves you and show you ways that you can change.

....

Jesus, thank You for Your love and kindness to me.
When I make mistakes, remind me that You love
me and that You'll never turn me away.

THE BEST BOOK EVER

*So My Word which goes from My mouth will
not return to Me empty. It will do what I want
it to do, and will carry out My plan well.*
ISAIAH 55:11

The Bible that you have in your home is an amazing tool from God. Inside it holds wonders, mysteries, miracles, adventures. . .and it's all true! But here is the most amazing thing: It is *alive*! Did you know that? God's Word is alive. The Bible tells us in Hebrews 4:12 that God's Word is living and active! Do you know of any other book like that ever written?

God's Word is how we get to know the truth about who God is and what He's done. It's how we begin to hear God's voice. The Holy Spirit uses words from the Bible to teach us God's will. And when you hide God's Word in your heart, you learn how to live a full and God-honoring life.

. . . .

*Wow, God. It's amazing that You sent us a book that
is alive and powerful. We worship You, not the book,
but thank You for loving us so much You gave us
an instruction manual to help us through life.*

A BIG DEAL

Give thanks to the Lord for He is good!
His loving-kindness lasts forever!
PSALM 107:1

There is no one else on this earth who can be faithful to you all the time. Not your parents, not your best friend, not people you trust from church. . .no one gets it right all the time. No one, that is, except Jesus.

And Jesus directs all His love and faithfulness right toward you. He will never leave you. He'll never give up on you. He'll never lie to you. He'll never ever stop loving you. Nothing you could ever do will change His mind about how much He loves you. That's a big deal! The biggest!

God looks at you and smiles because He sees Jesus in you. God is your loving friend and parent who never gets it wrong. You don't have to be afraid to talk to Him or tell Him what's going on in your life. He already knows, and He wants to hear from you anyway.

....

God, I want to know more about You, and I want
to grow closer to You each day. Thank You for
Your amazing love and faithfulness to me.

TAKING CARE OF GOD'S TEMPLE

Do you not know that your body is a house of God where the Holy Spirit lives? God gave you His Holy Spirit. Now you belong to God. You do not belong to yourselves. God bought you with a great price. So honor God with your body. You belong to Him.
1 Corinthians 6:19–20

You know that God's Spirit comes to live in you when you choose to follow Christ. The Bible actually calls your body a temple of the Holy Spirit. The secular dictionary defines a *temple* like this: "Any place or object in which God dwells, as the body of a Christian." Isn't that amazing?

So if your very own body is a place where God Himself dwells, doesn't that make you want to take care of it a little bit better? We can take care of our temples by eating right, exercising, getting enough rest, and keeping ourselves pure. Being a temple of the Holy Spirit is a big responsibility, and we can't do it without God's help. Ask for God's help to make healthy decisions for your body.

God, please help me take good care of my body, Your temple.

SPOTLESS AND BLAMELESS

Dear friends, since you are waiting for these things to happen, do all you can to be found by Him in peace. Be clean and free from sin.
2 PETER 3:14

The New International Version of the Bible says it like this: "Make every effort to be found spotless, blameless and at peace with him."

Being spotless and blameless sounds like such an impossible task, doesn't it? That's because it is. There is absolutely no way that you can keep yourself spotless and blameless in your own strength. If we could, we wouldn't need Jesus, right?

But God tells us that what is impossible with us, is possible with Him (Luke 18:27)! When God looks at you, He sees you as spotless and blameless because Jesus took all of your sin and made you perfectly clean.

The only way that you can live a spotless and blameless life in this confusing world is in the power of Jesus Christ Himself. He's the One at work in you.

....

God, I know there is no way I can be spotless and blameless on my own. I'm so thankful that You see me as clean and pure because of Jesus.

THE GREAT LIGHT

*You belong to God. He has done this for you
so you can tell others how God has called
you out of darkness into His great light.*
1 PETER 2:9

The enemy loves to keep people distracted and busy, fighting with one another in person or online, and spending most of their lives with screens in their faces instead of living a real, and abundant life.

And when evil gets ahold of people, they make really bad choices. That's why the light of Jesus is so important in our world today. . .and you have it! If you follow Jesus, He gives you His light so that you don't have to walk in darkness.

You don't have to follow the crowd into dark places. You can be a leader with a bright light that people will want to follow. They'll want to know what causes you to be joyful and loving. It's your job as a follower of Jesus to let your light shine as bright as possible!

....

*Jesus, please keep my light shining as bright
as possible. Help me to be a bright leader
in a distracted and dark world.*

*Watch your talk! No bad words should be coming
from your mouth. Say what is good. Your words
should help others grow as Christians.*
EPHESIANS 4:29

We've talked about how our words matter. Words can build people up or they can tear them down. Have you been affected by other people's words? Have you ever had someone you look up to say really nice things about you? It feels good, right? It makes you feel warm and loved and valued. Have you ever had someone say some really bad things about you? If so, you know how much it hurts.

Every time you speak to others, you can leave them feeling better or worse about themselves. You can encourage them and help them feel like they can be and do great things in life. . .or you can discourage them and leave them with bad thoughts. Pray for God to help you speak words that encourage others in a way that points them to the love of Jesus.

....

*God, please help me to build other people up and
encourage them with my words. I want to leave
them feeling loved, encouraged, and hopeful.*

LIVING WATERS

"The Holy Writings say that rivers of living water will flow from the heart of the one who puts his trust in Me."
JOHN 7:38

Isn't it cool to think that you have living water from Jesus flowing through you? What do you think Jesus wants to do with that water? Psalm 1:3 (NIV) tells us more about this: "That person is like a tree planted by streams of water, which yields its fruit in season and whose leaf does not wither—whatever they do prospers."

When you live your life for Jesus and allow Him to fill you with His living waters, you become like a healthy tree planted right by a stream and producing a lot of fruit. Trees that produce a lot of fruit can feed and bring joy to a lot of people. So can you! As you grow in your faith, Jesus will fill you with more and more living water to produce more and more spiritual fruit.

Jesus, I'm excited and thankful that You're filling me with living waters! Help me grow fruit that will bless my family and friends with Your love.

FOLLOW THE LEADER

As He saw many people, He had loving-pity on them.
They were troubled and were walking around everywhere.
They were like sheep without a shepherd.
MATTHEW 9:36

Sheep are born with an instinct to follow the leader. They will usually follow whatever the sheep in front of them are doing. If one sheep does something dangerous or stupid, the sheep behind it usually follow. It's even said that if one sheep jumps over a cliff, the rest of them will do it too.

When Jesus came to earth, He saw that the people were acting just like this. They were making bad choices and following those around them who were also making bad choices.

The Bible says that Jesus had compassion for these people. He knew what caused them to make those choices. He loved them and wanted to help. He came to be the Good Shepherd, to lead people to Himself. He showed how to love and to serve others with kindness and respect.

....

Jesus, thank You for showing me how to be a good leader.
Help me to lead others well as I follow You.

GOD SPEAKING THROUGH YOU

"Do not worry what you will say or how you will say it. The words will be given you when the time comes. It will not be you who will speak the words. The Spirit of your Father will speak through you."
MATTHEW 10:19–20

As a follower of Jesus, we're called to share our faith in Him with others. At some time in your life, you'll get a nudge from Jesus that you're supposed to say something about Him to someone else. This could happen at school, on the playground, in gymnastics class . . .anywhere. But this is not something to worry about. Want to know why? Because right here in this verse, Jesus says that the words you're supposed to say will be given to you.

If you ask Jesus for help, He'll give you the perfect thing to say or do at just the right time. And even if you feel like you've messed it up or said the wrong thing, don't worry about that either! Jesus can take what you've said or done and turn it into something good.

. . . .

Jesus, I'm so thankful I don't have to worry about any situation because You are always with me!

*You have never been tempted to sin in any different
way than other people. God is faithful. He will not
allow you to be tempted more than you can take.
But when you are tempted, He will make a
way for you to keep from falling into sin.*
1 CORINTHIANS 10:13

The New International Version of the Bible says it this way: "But when you are tempted, he will also provide a way out so that you can endure it."

Our enemy is out to trip up kids in any way he can. Telling you that you're not cool if you don't play the most popular video games, urging you to look at something you know you shouldn't online, convincing you to tell lies to get out of trouble.

Those are all tricks from the pit of hell. Don't fall for it! Instead, ask God to fill you up with His power to overcome all the tricks of the enemy. Ask the Holy Spirit to help you remember 1 Corinthians 10:13. God always provides a way out of temptation!

....

*God, please help me to look for the way out
every time I'm tempted to do the wrong thing.*

A REAL FRIENDSHIP WITH JESUS

"These people show respect to Me with their mouth, but their heart is far from Me. Their worship of Me is worth nothing. They teach what men have made up."
MATTHEW 15:8–9

The Pharisees in Jesus' day knew a lot about God and all of the Old Testament laws. In fact, they prided themselves on looking good on the outside and following all the laws strictly. They thought they knew everything about God, but they were actually very far from Him. People can say a lot of things, but it's what's inside their hearts that really matters. Remember that actions always speak louder than words.

Following Jesus doesn't mean following all of the rules and never messing up. Following Jesus means you have a real friendship with Him where you learn His Word and talk to Him about it. You get to know His heart and His love for you. You love Him back and you share that love with others.

Jesus, I want to know the real You. Bless our friendship, and remind me that You want to have conversations with me all day long.

THE COURAGE TO FOLLOW JESUS

Jesus said to His followers, "If anyone wants to be My follower, he must forget about himself. He must take up his cross and follow Me."
MATTHEW 16:24

Jesus tells us that to be His follower, we need to forget about ourselves and our needs. A true follower of Jesus is not a selfish person. He means that we need to trust God to take care of us instead of being worried about the stuff we think we need.

Back in Bible times, following Jesus was a dangerous thing to do. The disciples risked everything to follow Jesus, and the kingdom of God has spread to all the nations because of it. What is Jesus asking you to do to help grow His kingdom? If Jesus' disciples trusted Jesus with their lives, can you trust Jesus to help you share His love with a friend in need? Ask Him to give you the kind of faith where you trust Jesus for everything—your food, your safety, your very life.

....

Jesus, please give me the courage to help grow Your kingdom by sharing my faith with others. I trust You to take care of me!

RICHES AND GENEROSITY

"Do not gather together for yourself riches of this earth. They will be eaten by bugs and become rusted. Men can break in and steal them. Gather together riches in heaven where they will not be eaten by bugs or become rusted. Men cannot break in and steal them. For wherever your riches are, your heart will be there also."
MATTHEW 6:19–21

God wants us to seek Him, not money and things that don't last. As you grow up, you'll see more and more that most people chase after things that don't last like money, clothes, electronics, and a lot of other "things" that don't really matter. But the truth is chasing after all of that will never fill you up and make you truly happy. Only God can meet the deep longings in your heart.

Ask God to plant seeds of generosity in your heart. Look out for the needs of others around you and see how God wants you to help.

. . . .

Lord, please give me a generous heart where I think of others and their needs before my own. Show me how to help the people around me who need something.

MUSTARD-SEED FAITH

"For sure, I tell you, if you have faith as a mustard seed, you will say to this mountain, 'Move from here to over there,' and it would move over. You will be able to do anything."
MATTHEW 17:20

The disciples were having a hard time getting a job done. They weren't so sure about this new power that Jesus had given them. Jesus reminded them that it was the power of God working inside them that gave them the ability to get the job done, not their own power. The same is true for us.

Jesus reminded His followers about mustard-seed faith. Mustard seeds are super tiny but grow into trees. When we have small faith in a huge God, anything is possible! Jesus is calling us to have that kind of faith too. Our part is trusting that Jesus is all-powerful and can do anything. God's part is to be exactly who He is: all-powerful and faithful.

Jesus, I trust You to be faithful and all-powerful in my life. Though my faith is small, I know that Your power is big!

SINGING FOREVER

I will sing of the loving-kindness of the Lord forever. I will make known with my mouth how faithful You are to all people. For I said, "Loving-kindness will be built up forever. You will make known how faithful You are in the heavens."
PSALM 89:1–2

God shows His love for us in so many ways. One of the simplest ways to actually see God's love is to go outside and experience His works for yourself.

You can see His handiwork in the flowers and trees in spring and summer. The bright leaves changing in the fall and the blankets of snow He sends in the winter. The skies tell of His wonders in every season. Animals and creatures great and small know their Creator. The birds God created are always singing His praises as they go about their busy tasks. . .and you can too.

God gave you your voice to talk to Him, to tell of His great love and to sing His praises every day of your life.

. . . .

I love to sing, God. Even if I'm not that good at it. Help me to never quit telling the story of Your love. . .or singing about it.

> *"Are not two small birds sold for a very small piece of money? And yet not one of the birds falls to the earth without your Father knowing it. God knows how many hairs you have on your head. So do not be afraid. You are more important than many small birds."*
> MATTHEW 10:29–31

Check out what the Bible says about you in Psalm 139:13–14 (NIV): "For you created my inmost being; you knit me together in my mother's womb. I praise you because I am fearfully and wonderfully made; your works are wonderful, I know that full well." Can you imagine that? It's all true.

Imagine Jesus putting you together as you were growing in your mom's tummy. He knows everything about you, and He cares for you more than anything else in creation. You are so important to Him that He died for you on the cross so that you could be with Him forever. The next time you're feeling down or unimportant. . .remember who made you and how much He loves you!

....

Jesus, thank You for loving me so much. You made me and I'm important. . .simply because You said so!

GROWING IN FAITH THROUGH MENTORSHIP

*Let us help each other to love others and to do
good. Let us not stay away from church meetings.
Some people are doing this all the time. Comfort each
other as you see the day of His return coming near.*
HEBREWS 10:24–25

Do you know what a mentor or an accountability partner is? It's someone who is usually older than you who loves God and is willing to teach you some things about being a follower of Jesus. As you get older, you might pray about finding a mentor to help you on your faith journey.

A mentor or an accountability partner needs to be a safe person who your parents know about. This person should be dependable so that you can plan on meeting together regularly to talk about God and pray together.

Is this something you might like to do to get closer to God? Make a list with your parents of several godly people who come to mind. Pray for God to direct you to a trustworthy person who can encourage you and help you grow in the faith.

. . . .

*Lord, please direct me to a wise
mentor to help me grow in my faith.*

"The time is coming, yes, it is here now, when the true worshipers will worship the Father in spirit and in truth. The Father wants that kind of worshipers."
JOHN 4:23

When we worship God in Spirit, it means that we are worshipping from our hearts from anywhere. We don't have to go to a church or be with other people to worship God in Spirit. We can do it right from our own rooms.

The Message translation helps us understand what this verse means a bit more: "That's the kind of people the Father is out looking for: those who are simply and honestly themselves before him in their worship. God is sheer being itself—Spirit. Those who worship him must do it out of their very being, their spirits, their true selves, in adoration" (verses 23–24).

When we worship God in truth, it means that we're honestly being ourselves before God. We aren't hiding anything or pretending to be something we're not.

....

Jesus, help me to be honest and true when I worship You. Thank You that I can come to You from anywhere. . . at home, at school, even my own bed!

GOD'S FAITHFUL LOVE

Praise the Lord, all nations! Praise Him, all people!
For His loving-kindness toward us is great. And the
truth of the Lord lasts forever. Praise the Lord!
PSALM 117:1–2

All throughout the book of Psalms in the Bible you will
hear verses like that one. Here are a couple more:

- *"Give thanks to the LORD, for he is good! His faithful*
  love endures forever" (Psalm 136:1 NLT).
- *"Give thanks to him who alone does mighty miracles.*
  His faithful love endures forever" (Psalm 136:4 NLT).

You'll find evidence of God's faithful love all through
the Bible. In fact, that's really what it's all about.

God's love is faithful and will last even when everyone else's love fades away. Jesus is the One you can
turn to at all times. He wants to celebrate with you in
good times and comfort you in bad times. When everyone else is on your case, He will lovingly stand beside
you and lead you into His truth and grace. You'll never
have a better friend than Jesus.

. . . .

Thank You again and again for Your great love for
me, Lord. I believe You are faithful and that You'll
always love me and be with me no matter what.

A BRAND-NEW HEART

*"I will give you a new heart and put a new
spirit within you. I will take away your heart
of stone and give you a heart of flesh."*
EZEKIEL 36:26

We've been talking about how God gives us His Spirit when we choose to commit our lives to Christ. God sets a brand-new heart in each of us. Romans 8:9 (NLT) says: "But you are not controlled by your sinful nature. You are controlled by the Spirit if you have the Spirit of God living in you. (And remember that those who do not have the Spirit of Christ living in them do not belong to him at all.)"

God removes our old stubborn and sinful heart and gives us a soft and tender heart that wants the ways of Jesus in our lives. Do you wish He would do that for some of your friends and family too? Go back to page 53 and remember to pray for them regularly.

....

*God, thanks for my new heart. I pray for my friends and
family who aren't fully Yours yet. Please give them
a new heart, and help them desire to live for You.*

AN IMPORTANT REMINDER

We know that God makes all things work
together for the good of those who love Him
and are chosen to be a part of His plan.
ROMANS 8:28

Sometimes we need a good reminder of what God is doing in our lives. So here it is: God is with you always. He is listening, and He loves you like you're the only kid in the universe! You are His child, and He will never abandon you. You are a child of the King of all kings, and He has wonderful plans for your life. Even the painful things that happen in life, God will miraculously turn into good things if you trust in Him!

As you grow up, you're going to have a lot of distractions in life, trying to get you to turn away from trusting in God's great love for you. That's our enemy's one purpose in this life. So remember how much God loves you and hide this verse in your heart. Memorize it and allow the Holy Spirit to bring it to your mind anytime you start to forget.

God, I pray that You would keep me
from getting too distracted in this life.
Thank You for Your loving reminders.

THE PERFECT PARENT

*So the Lord wants to show you kindness. He waits
on high to have loving-pity on you. For the Lord
is a God of what is right and fair. And good
will come to all those who hope in Him.*
Isaiah 30:18

Have you ever longed for something? It's where you want something so bad you can hardly wait until it happens. The New International Version of this verse says, "The Lord longs to be gracious to you." God does not force Himself on anyone. That was never His plan. He has made it clear who He is and what He's done. . .and then He waits for us to come to Him.

God's desire is to shower you with love and compassion, but He won't do it unless you let Him. And He longs for you to let Him bless You. Everything that happens to you in this life can be used for your good and God's glory. Imagine a parent that loves you unconditionally and never ever makes a mistake. That's who God is.

. . . .

*Thank You for being my perfect parent.
I choose to come to You each day,
knowing You want the very best for me.*

A CLEAN HEART

Make a clean heart in me, O God.
Give me a new spirit that will not be moved.
PSALM 51:10

You don't have to be perfect to have a personal relationship with God. In the Old Testament, King David messed up big-time, and yet He was still called a "man after God's own heart."

Psalm 51 was written by David after he had sinned against God. The prophet Nathan had to go to David to get him to see what he was doing wrong. After David realized his sin, he wrote Psalm 51. Open your Bible and read the entire thing.

Have you ever felt this way? Like you've messed up really bad and you need a clean heart? Pray Psalm 51 to God and ask Him to clean out your heart. Through Jesus, God wipes our sin clean and makes our hearts whiter than snow (verse 7).

God, I've messed up. I still want to be a kid after
Your own heart, Lord. Please forgive my sin,
and give me a clean heart. Thank You for Jesus
and that through Him, I am right with You.

LET THE SPIRIT CHANGE YOU

*This has become my way of life: When I want to do what
is right, I always do what is wrong. My mind and heart
agree with the Law of God. But there is a different law
at work deep inside of me that fights with my mind.
This law of sin holds me in its power because sin is still in me.*
ROMANS 7:21–23

Does this scripture sound a little familiar to you? You've
decided that you'll never do something again, and then
you find yourself doing that very same thing. . .again.
You get so mad at yourself each time it happens and
you feel like you are a complete failure! But remember that Jesus already paid for all of your mistakes. . .
past. . .present. . .future.

When sin happens again and again. . .take it straight
to God. Confess it and tell Him how you really feel.
Ask Him to take control of your life and allow the Spirit
of God to change you.

*God, I want to do Your will. I'm not getting
some things right, and I need Your help. Please
fill me with Your Spirit and change my heart.*

LOVING GOD BACK

*God has shown His love to us by sending His only Son
into the world. God did this so we might have life
through Christ. This is love! It is not that we loved
God but that He loved us. For God sent His Son
to pay for our sins with His own blood.*
1 John 4:9–10

Sometimes it's hard to know how to love God back after such a sacrifice. His great love can be overwhelming! But when we follow God's Word, listen for His voice, and love others. . .that is how we show love to God.

But what about those times when we aren't sure that we are loving God very well? "We know and rely on the love God has for us" (1 John 4:16 NIV). The only way we can love at all is because He loved us first. He is the author of love, and He'll continue to show us how to love better and better as we follow Him.

*God, please help me to listen for Your
voice in my life and to follow after You,
relying on the love You have for me.*

LOVE IS A CHOICE

Love does not give up. Love is kind. Love is not jealous. Love does not put itself up as being important. Love has no pride. Love does not do the wrong thing. Love never thinks of itself. Love does not get angry. Love does not remember the suffering that comes from being hurt by someone. Love is not happy with sin. Love is happy with the truth. Love takes everything that comes without giving up. Love believes all things. Love hopes for all things. Love keeps on in all things.
1 Corinthians 13:4–7

Did you know that the biblical definition of *love* is God? God = love. Love = God. First John 4:17 (MSG) says: "God is love. When we take up permanent residence in a life of love, we live in God and God lives in us." First Corinthians 13 tells us a little bit more of what love is.

Most people think love is a feeling, but that's not always true. Love is a choice. You can still choose to love someone even if you don't feel like it.

God, please help me to choose to love even when I don't feel like it.

OLD AND YOUNG

*He took the children in His arms. He put His hands
on them and prayed that good would come to them.*
MARK 10:16

Criticism is when someone judges you, usually in a negative way. People were often criticizing Jesus because they thought He should be doing what they wanted Him to do. The Pharisees, and sometimes even Jesus' own friends, were critical of the people He chose to spend time with.

Back in Bible times, women and children weren't considered very important. In fact, they were often treated as property. This was not God's plan. Jesus came to show another way. He loved women and children and spent lots of time with them. Jesus was offended when the disciples tried to keep children away from Him. He told the disciples not to prevent kids from coming. He honored women and children and made them feel important. He said that "anyone who will not receive the kingdom of God like a little child will never enter it" (Mark 10:15 NIV). The faith of children is pure and strong. They believe someone who feels safe to them. Jesus wants all of His children, old and young, to have faith like that!

. . . .

*I'm so thankful that I'm important to You, Jesus.
Your love for me is so amazing! I know I'm safe with You.*

Dear Christian friends, do not believe every spirit.
But test the spirits to see if they are from God for
there are many false preachers in the world.
1 JOHN 4:1

The Message translation says this: "Don't believe everything you hear. Carefully weigh and examine what people tell you. Not everyone who talks about God comes from God."

Remember that the enemy likes to trick people. And he's really good at it. He likes to deceive, and the Bible says that he even disguises himself as an angel of light (2 Corinthians 11:14).

Some people who have been tricked like to take certain verses out of the Bible and use them to say what they want to say. So always test what people say about God with His Word. Look it up. Find a study Bible or an online study Bible and find out what God's Word really says.

You have the Spirit of God right there in your heart, so if someone says something about God and it doesn't quite feel right, check it out.

. . . .

God, please give me wisdom about You.
Thank You that I have Your Spirit to guide me.

SHARING OUR SADNESS

*If we are children of God, we will receive everything
He has promised us. We will share with Christ all the
things God has given to Him. But we must share His
suffering if we are to share His shining-greatness.*
ROMANS 8:17

A broken heart, a friend lets you down, a problem at school, a pet or someone you love dies or moves away . . .life can be tough. When we go through times of sadness in our lives, we have the opportunity to get closer to Christ and share the suffering. . .or push God away and become bitter.

Have you ever seen a beautiful bitter person? Probably not. When we allow bitterness to consume us, it can start to turn us ugly from the inside out. But when we share our sufferings with Christ and allow Him to fill us with His peace and presence, His light shines in the darkest places. . .filling us with His kind of beauty.

So when life is tough, ask Jesus to fill you up. He will provide everything you need to live this life with joy.

....

*Jesus, please shine Your light into the dark places in
my life. I want to be filled with Your light and love.*

"It must be preached that men must be sorry for their sins and turn from them. Then they will be forgiven. This must be preached in His name to all nations beginning in Jerusalem. You are to tell what you have seen."
LUKE 24:47–48

Jesus wants us to tell others about what we've seen Him do. He told the disciples to tell everyone about everything they saw and heard from Jesus. He wants us to share what He is doing in our lives too. People want to know that a friendship with Jesus makes a difference in their lives.

Take some time and write down what you've been praying for and how God has answered you. How has Jesus changed your life? Sharing this is called sharing your story or your testimony. A testimony is your personal story about Jesus and what you've seen Him do in your life. Write down how you first came to know Jesus and what He's been doing in your life since then. Your testimony about Jesus is powerful and important.

....

Jesus, thank You for all the amazing things You've done in my life. Use my testimony to bring other people to know You.

*Everything that was written in the Holy Writings long
ago was written to teach us. By not giving up, God's
Word gives us strength and hope. Now the God Who helps
you not to give up and gives you strength will help you
think so you can please each other as Christ Jesus did.*
ROMANS 15:4–5

You have a choice every day when you wake up. You can
choose to be thankful for a new day and look at it with
joy and hopeful expectation, or you can choose to let
the day get ahead of you and spend the rest of the day
trying to catch up.

Ask God to help you see each new day as a gift.
As you wake up, ask Him to go before you and remind
you that God's Spirit is always with you. Then, even if
you're headed to a dreaded dentist appointment, you'll
be able to see the little blessings that God sends your
way as you look for Him.

*God, please help me choose to see
each day and each moment as a gift.
Change my attitude to be like Yours.*

IMPOSSIBLE HOPE

When the Lord saw her, He had loving-pity for her and said, "Do not cry." He went and put His hand on the box in which the dead man was carried. The men who were carrying it, stopped. Jesus said, "Young man, I say to you, get up!" The man who was dead sat up and began to talk. Then Jesus gave him to his mother.

LUKE 7:13–15

A young man was dead, and he was being carried through the town. His mom was sad and probably scared about the future. But what could be done? Her son was already dead.

But then Jesus saw her. The Bible tells us that His heart went out to her. He had compassion and love for this widow who had lost her only son. He told her not to cry, and then He commanded the dead man to get up—and he did!

Jesus can take a completely hopeless situation and turn it around. Whenever you feel like a problem is completely impossible, remember that Jesus can do anything!

....

*Jesus, help me to trust that You
can bring hope to any situation.*

SEASONS OF LIFE

For His anger lasts only a short time. But His favor is for life. Crying may last for a night, but joy comes with the new day.
PSALM 30:5

Just like we have winter, spring, summer, and fall—each bringing something new and necessary to our world—we also have different seasons of life. God's Word tells us, "There is a time for everything, and a season for every activity under the heavens" (Ecclesiastes 3:1 NIV).

You may be in a spring season of life right now, going through a lot of changes as you sprout and grow. But even if you're in a cold, wintry season that doesn't seem very fun. . .always remember, it's just a season. It will soon pass away, bringing with it a new and different season. Allow these thoughts to bring you comfort. The hard stuff might last for a season, but joy is just around the corner.

. . . .

God, please help me to get through hard days knowing that this is only a season and that You offer constant peace and joy in Your presence. Thank You for the different seasons of my life. Use them to make me more like You.

It is because of the Lord's loving-kindness that we
are not destroyed for His loving-pity never ends.
It is new every morning. He is so very faithful.
LAMENTATIONS 3:22–23

God's love never ends. . .and neither does His mercy. Do you know what *mercy* means? Mercy is the true fact that God doesn't punish us as our sins deserve. Grace is when God gives us something that we don't deserve (like forgiveness and special blessings). Mercy is when God chooses not to give us something we do deserve (punishment for sin). He does this because of what Jesus did for us on the cross.

The Bible tells us that God's mercies are new every morning. So if you feel like you've made a bunch of mistakes today, talk to God about them. Ask Him to forgive you and give you a pure heart. Then go to sleep in peace knowing that our great God forgives you and loves you. God is always ready to give you a fresh start.

....

Thank You, God, for a fresh start each day.
Help me to follow You with my whole heart today.

GOD IS GREAT

*"Tell of His great works among all the people.
For great is the Lord. He is to be given much praise.
And He is to be honored with fear more than all gods.
For all the gods of the people are false gods. But the
Lord made the heavens. Honor and great power are
with Him. Strength and joy are in His place."*
1 CHRONICLES 16:24–27

If you go to a public school and have friends who don't follow Jesus, you already know that there are tons of different beliefs out there. People make up their own gods these days. A god or idol can be anything that someone worships with his or her time and attention.

The difference is that our God is a real, living God. The only true God. He still performs wonders and miracles every single day. Do you know where to look for them? Ask for God to give you eyes to see His wondrous miracles and blessings all around you. . .then watch and trust that He is working in your life.

. . . .

*God, You are great. You are worthy of all my attention.
Open my eyes to see You at work in my heart.*

BE THE BOOK

*I will give thanks to the Lord with all my heart. I will
tell of all the great things You have done. I will be
glad and full of joy because of You. I will sing
praise to Your name, O Most High.*
PSALM 9:1–2

Have you heard the saying "You are the only Bible that
some people will ever read"? That means that some
people you'll meet during this lifetime have never
opened a Bible before. But God put them in your
path so that you can be a living, breathing example of
God's Word.

Are you writing the book of God's wonders in
your life? Not literally. . .you don't really have to write
a book. You can *be* the book! When you live out a life
of joy and thankfulness. . .other people are going to
wonder what is different about you. That makes you a
real-life, walking Bible to someone else.

You have an amazing opportunity every day to
make a difference in the lives of everyone you meet.
The only smile that person might see the whole day
could be from you.

....

*God, help me make a difference in
the life of someone else today.*

BACKWARD AND UPSIDE DOWN

"The person who is not trying to honor himself will be made important."
MATTHEW 23:12

There is a theme in Jesus' words. They seem completely backward and upside down from what our world believes now: We love others by serving them. The first shall be last and the last shall be first. The humble person will be lifted up. Being great comes from serving others.

Many kids today are focused on how many likes they can get on their social media accounts or YouTube videos. They're upset when they don't get enough traffic to their posts. Even really young kids! But Jesus says here that the person who is not trying to get the most attention will be made important. The kids scrambling to try and become famous aren't living the life Jesus wants for them.

If you spend your life in the service of Jesus and others, you will find that your heart is overflowing with joy. And it won't matter how many likes you get from people you don't even know!

....

Jesus, please forgive me when I worry about how many people like me. I want to find joy in serving You and others.

FOLLOWING THE WAY OF PEACE

Turn away from what is sinful. Do what is good. Look for peace and follow it. The eyes of the Lord are on those who do what is right and good. His ears are open to their cry.
PSALM 34:14–15

When we obey God by being thankful and not worrying, He gives us true and lasting peace. But it doesn't stay like that forever! We have to keep giving our worries to God and replacing them with thankfulness. . .every . . .single. . .day. It's definitely not just a onetime thing.

And if we want God to watch over us and hear our prayers, we've got to keep away from evil and do good. The Bible says that we need to turn away from evil. . . to actually stop and go the other direction. We can't just assume that trouble won't find us if we're not looking for it.

Our enemy is constantly looking for ways to get us to turn away from God (1 Peter 5:8) and destroy our peace. Ask God to help you turn and go the other way so you can keep your eyes on Christ.

God, please help me to turn away
from evil and to seek You in all things.

GOD'S THOUGHTS

"For My thoughts are not your thoughts, and My ways are not your ways," says the Lord. "For as the heavens are higher than the earth, so are My ways higher than your ways, and My thoughts than your thoughts."
ISAIAH 55:8–9

The Bible tells us that God's ways are not our ways. We can only think with our human minds. . .but God is the One who made them! We can't possibly know all His ways or understand all His plans.

If someone tells you something about God and you're not sure if it is true or not, remember that the best thing to do is to go talk to God yourself. Get into His Word and get to know Him. One of the best books of the Bible to start knowing God is the book of John. Try reading it yourself this month. Ask God to come alongside you as you read it and give you wisdom.

God, I'm so amazed that You want me to have a personal relationship with You! I can't thank You enough for allowing me to come straight to You with all my questions. Thank You for guiding me!

GREAT PLANS

The Lord will finish the work He started for me.
O Lord, Your loving-kindness lasts forever.
Do not turn away from the works of Your hands.
PSALM 138:8

You were put on this earth for a purpose. You didn't happen by accident, and the Bible tells us that God knows the number of your days and the number of hairs on your head. Yes, you were brought into this world by your parents, but it is God who determines your purpose.

Philippians 1:6 (NLT) says, "And I am certain that God, who began the good work within you, will continue his work until it is finally finished on the day when Christ Jesus returns." God started a good work in you the day you were born. He has great plans for your life (Jeremiah 29:11–13) and wants to be with you every step of the way. Seek Him for every decision, big or small. . .He wants to walk with you through them all.

....

God, thanks for creating me! I'm so glad You know
everything about me and want to help me with all
my decisions. Fill me with Your Holy Spirit and
guide me closer and closer to Your heart.

LIVE IN PEACE

As much as you can,
live in peace with all men.
Romans 12:18

There are definitely days where you might not feel like living at peace with everyone. Maybe you didn't sleep well and you wake up grumpy. Or maybe you have no idea why you are annoyed—you just are—and you want people to leave you alone for a while.

The best thing to do when you feel like that is to find a quiet place just to be with God. Kindly ask your friends and family to give you a little space, and go talk to God about the way you're feeling. Even if you don't understand why you feel the way you do. . .God does! So take your problems to Him first and allow Him to help you sort them out. Ask Him to change your attitude as He works on your heart. Then you can enjoy peaceful relationships with others because you know that the God who created you is working on your problems with you.

. . . .

God, sometimes I can get pretty grumpy with other people. Please forgive me for that and help me to take my thoughts and feelings to You first.

LOVING YOUR NEIGHBOR

"Which of these three do you think was a neighbor to the man who was beaten by the robbers?" The man who knew the Law said, "The one who showed loving-pity on him." Then Jesus said, "Go and do the same."
LUKE 10:36–37

Jesus tells a story about the good Samaritan. A man was beaten and left for dead by robbers. Three people walked by the hurting man. The first two saw the man and passed by on the other side. The third man went to the wounded man and helped him. He bandaged his wounds and took him to an inn to heal, paying for his expenses. Which man acted like a good neighbor to the wounded man? The one who helped of course.

What does this story mean to you? Who is your neighbor? Is it just your friends and the people you love? No, Jesus says that anyone we come across is our neighbor. And Jesus wants us to love our neighbors as ourselves. Sometimes that is difficult! Especially if you have weird neighbors! But Jesus can help you love even the unlovable. Just ask!

....

Jesus, please help me love my neighbors in ways that bless You. Even when it's hard.

NO MATTER WHAT OTHERS THINK

A woman came with a jar of perfume.
She had given much money for this. As Jesus
ate, she poured the perfume on His head.
MATTHEW 26:7

While Jesus was eating with His disciples, His friend Mary came and poured expensive perfume on His head. That sounds a little strange, right? The disciples didn't understand what she was doing and criticized her for it. Jesus defended Mary and told the disciples what a beautiful thing it was that she had done. She had honored Him. Jesus understood her heart.

Sometimes it's hard to do something that we believe Jesus is asking us to do. Especially if other people are around. But Jesus will defend you and take care of you as you carry out His plans for your life.

Jesus said that this special story of Mary would be told all throughout the world, and you're hearing it right now too.

. . . .

Jesus, help me be strong and confident in my faith
as I live my life for You. Even when other people think
my faith is strange or weird. I know You are with me.

SHARING MY BLESSINGS

*"For I was hungry and you gave Me food to eat.
I was thirsty and you gave Me water to drink.
I was a stranger and you gave Me a room."*
MATTHEW 25:35

Serving others means that you put their needs above your own; you find out what they need and you do your best to help them.

Did you know that when you serve others you are actually serving Jesus? Matthew 25:40 (NIV) says, "Truly I tell you, whatever you did for one of the least of these brothers and sisters of mine, you did for me."

Sit down with your family and think about ways you can get involved with needy people in your community. Most communities have a soup kitchen, and many churches stock up on supplies to help people in need. Find out how you can help and remember that you're serving Jesus as you do it!

....

*Jesus, I want to help take care of needs in
my community. Thank You for Your blessings!
Help me share these blessings with those in need.*

"Come to Me, all of you who work and have heavy loads. I will give you rest. Follow My teachings and learn from Me. I am gentle and do not have pride. You will have rest for your souls. For My way of carrying a load is easy and My load is not heavy."
MATTHEW 11:28–30

Jesus wants you to come to Him about every...single... thing. He wants to share your whole life with you. The good, the bad, the easy and fun, the difficult and heavy. He offers to give your soul a rest. A deep soul-rest is the kind you need when you're really tired from trying to make everyone happy.

The Message translation of the Bible says: "Come to me. Get away with me and you'll recover your life. . . . I won't lay anything heavy or ill-fitting on you. Keep company with me and you'll learn to live freely and lightly." Living freely and lightly sounds pretty good, right? So come to Him. Bring Him all your thoughts and feelings.

. . . .

Jesus, I want to share my whole life with You. Show me how to live freely and lightly without trying to please everyone else.

> *Jesus came and said to them, "All power has been given to Me in heaven and on earth. Go and make followers of all the nations. Baptize them in the name of the Father and of the Son and of the Holy Spirit. Teach them to do all the things I have told you. And I am with you always, even to the end of the world."*
> MATTHEW 28:18–20

These famous last words of Jesus are also known as the Great Commission. A commission is when you trust someone else enough to give that person special power and authority. This commission was for the disciples, but it is also for us still today. Jesus wants us to share His love with everyone and pass on the truth of Jesus to them.

Jesus promised to be with us always. He sent us His Holy Spirit to be alive and at work in us, to help us and give us courage. The Holy Spirit will help us carry out Jesus' Great Commission.

....

Jesus, thank You for Your promise to always be with me. Give me help and courage to share about You with those around me.

THE ONLY THING THAT COUNTS

But faith working through love is important.
GALATIANS 5:6

Mother Teresa said, "Let us always meet each other with a smile, for the smile is the beginning of love." Can you try that today? Even if you really don't feel like smiling, remember to be the light in someone else's dark world.

The New International Version of Galatians 5:6 says: "The only thing that counts is faith expressing itself through love."

Ask God to fill you with His love today so that you can share a smile with everyone you meet. The Bible promises that when we are weak, God is strong (2 Corinthians 12:9–10). So if you're feeling down and you don't have a smile left to share, remember that God can be your strength for you. He can help you love like Jesus loved. And that's the only thing that really counts.

. . . .

God, sometimes I get so caught up in my own feelings that I forget what really matters. Your love! That's it! That's what You put me here for: to love You and to love others. Be my strength today and help me love people through You.

SCRIPTURE INDEX

OLD TESTAMENT